SHARED CROSSING

THE FINAL JOURNEY

A Memoir

DEBORAH HARKIN

atmosphere press

Published by Atmosphere Press

Cover design by Ronaldo Alves

Atmospherepress.com

Praise for SHARED CROSSING: The Final Journey

"A truly beautiful book! Deborah Harkin takes on the big existential questions about dying, death, and life itself as she unfolds her intimate end-of-life journey with her beloved mother. She leaves no stone unturned in her thoughtful, tender, and riveting account. Dr. Harkin offers the reader a groundbreaking perspective for living life's final chapter with a forgotten wisdom and courageous love. Put your seat belt on as this deeply honest memoir will bring you to tears, unexpected joy, and sublime peace!"

– William Peters, MFT
Founder of the Shared Crossing Project,
and author of *At Heaven's Door*

"Eloquent and moving. A deep dive into the gifts and challenges of caregiving and accompanying the dying. Read this book—you will laugh, you will cry and you will be grateful."

– Dr. Monica Williams
Emergency Physician and author of *It's OK to Die*

"Deborah Harkin's book brings into sharp focus that spiritual experiences are mysteries to be appreciated rather than events to be explained. Deborah's journey to embrace her own experiences around end of life can serve as a model for readers to be more receptive to those elusive moments of transcendence and wonder."

– Michael Kinsella, Ph.D.
Hospice Spiritual Counselor and Religious Studies Scholar

I write in honor of all caregivers—family, friends, volunteers, and professionals, with special thanks to the Shared Crossing Project.

TABLE OF CONTENTS

INTRODUCTION

"Listen, O drop, give yourself up without regret,
and in exchange gain the Ocean."

—*Rumi*

"Shared crossing" is a term that has come to describe extraordinary experiences that can be shared between the living and the dying towards the end of life—and perhaps a glimpse of what lies beyond.

I hold a Ph.D. in psychology and have had the good fortune to work with William Peters, founder of the Shared Crossing Project, since its inception at the Family Therapy Institute in Santa Barbara. I was in my third or fourth career and a psychotherapy intern when I began assisting in William's workshops in what was an entirely new field for me. I immediately saw the benefit of education surrounding the existing literature on end of life, and I absorbed the richness of experiences shared within the groups. For me, talking about death has always been about life. Oddly enough—enlivening. What I did not know at the time was that this work would profoundly prepare me for the journey I would soon take with my mother.

Confronting death touches into life's deepest mysteries—

What is the source and meaning of life?

Why are we here now, in this form, as human?

What is the nature of consciousness?

What is the relationship between matter and spirit?

What is our individual and communal place within the universe ...

And what lies beyond?

On less heady ground, the subject of death is fraught with fear. Fear of the loss of a loved one ... the awkwardness of what to say to those who have. Buried, or not, fears around our own death. The specter of death confronts us with our own mortality and cuts to the very core of the most human of questions—what happens when I die?

We, as a culture, are both terrified and fascinated by death.

My purpose in writing about the experiences surrounding my mother's death is a personal one. I have learned the importance of talking about death. Not talking about it leaves us in fear, in uncertainty, and very much alone. In addition, stories of near-death and shared death experiences often focus on the extraordinary occurrences that are possible, vivid, and real. (The word *phenomena* is only one letter away from phenomenal!) The road that brought us there can be overlooked, along with its hidden treasures.

Experiences around the end of life, grief, and mourning

are different for each person—shaped by the circumstances of the death, cultural traditions, beliefs, family dynamics, personalities, individual histories, and closeness to or distance from the dying or deceased person. My story is only my own.

I write my story in honor of my mother, as well as my sisters and father, who walked this path—although at a distance—by my side. It is my hope that it can be read with the pain, joy, love, and light with which it is written.

Mine is a hybrid memoir in which I wear the hats of psychotherapist, educator, student of life, and—most importantly—daughter. My work with the Shared Crossing Project provided a wealth of information that sparked my curiosity and helped shape interactions with my mother. Becoming familiar with some of the phenomena common towards the end of life can make them less confusing or frightening when they occur, ease fears around our own death—and teach us much about how to be with the dying.

———

Some of the language and concepts that have emerged from end-of-life studies may help you to understand my story differently—and perhaps your own.

Near-Death Experiences (NDEs)

Near-death experiences, commonly referred to as NDEs, pave the way to understanding experiences that can be shared between the living and the dying. Many features of

NDEs also appear in accounts of shared death experiences.

A near-death experience is a deeply personal one, as told by an individual who has come close to death and survived. These experiences are usually due to a serious accident or life-threatening illness, but may also occur during an attempted suicide. Near-death experiences vary and are unique to each person. However, similar elements can be found even across cultures.

Most people are familiar with near-death experiences as portrayed in film or literature. The dying person may hear "heavenly music" as they move through a tunnel and "towards the light." Scenes of their life "flash before their eyes." They may also enter into an indescribably beautiful landscape. The person inevitably reaches a turning point—a border or boundary which they cannot move beyond—they are then catapulted back into their body. These words and images may seem like artful fabrications, or cliché, but they are based on actual near-death experiences. In truth, reports of NDEs are far more complex and diverse. (See the Appendix for more detailed information on end-of-life studies and near-death experiences.)

Neuroscientists sometimes attempt to explain near-death experiences as creations of the mind—as coping mechanisms or the result of physiological changes in the body and brain during the death process. Others will understand NDEs as a window into another realm, a glimpse of the afterlife—or as an essential truth of existence, our eternal oneness with God.

While NDEs may be explained, in part, by physiological changes during the dying process, shared death experiences cannot be dismissed so easily.

Shared Death Experiences (SDEs)

Extraordinary end-of-life phenomena have been documented since the end of the nineteenth century by the Society for Psychical Research in London. In 1926, Sir William Barrett published the first study on "deathbed visions," based on accounts not only by the dying but loved ones and caregivers as well.

The term "shared death experience" was popularized in Dr. Raymond Moody's 2010 book (with Paul Perry), *Glimpses of Eternity*. Shared death experiences (SDEs) refer to reports by a healthy bystander—usually a loved one or caregiver—who feels they have observed or participated in the initial stages of the dying person's transition from life into death.

Shared death experiences may occur while awake or asleep. Many experiencers report being visited by a loved one as they passed. This may include sensing their presence, dreaming or having visions of the dying person's movement towards a destination—often a transcendent light. Some accounts include sharing in a life review, encounters with spirit guides, or a greeting party—even accompanying the dying as they enter a beautiful and blissful realm. As in near-death experiences, they reach a point at which they must return.

Shared death experiences usually occur close to the time of death but may happen moments, hours, days, or even weeks before or after the death. Some SDEs take place at the bedside; however, many stories come from individuals who were at a distance from the dying person at their end of life. This speaks to the depth and breadth of connections we share with others—not limited by the bounds of time and space.

Although shared death experiences may be the most remarkable of end-of-life phenomena, they are only one aspect of experiences that can be shared between the living and the dying.

Shared Crossings

As described by the Shared Crossing Project, shared crossings are experiences that convey information about an impending death and suggest the continuation of consciousness after bodily death.

These phenomena are the subject of ongoing study by the Shared Crossing Research Initiative directed by William Peters and conducted by Chief of Research, Dr. Michael Kinsella, and their team. Based on the research, Peters has identified a full spectrum of end-of-life experiences that may be reported by the dying and/or the living—loved ones, caregivers, or even a bystander. As a result, these experiences can be spoken between them and are often healing and profound.

Phenomena associated with shared crossings include: Pre-death premonitions, pre- and post-death visions and visitations, synchronicities (unusual events that hold personal significance), terminal lucidity (during which the dying person rallies and is able to communicate), and shared death experiences, as well as direct post-death communication. Detailed descriptions of each are available on the

Shared Crossing Project website (www.sharedcrossing.com), along with excerpts from research transcripts and a video library.

Consistent themes and patterns appear in SDEs and shared crossings. However, the stories are compelling precisely because they are so unexpected and deeply personal.

Discussion of NDEs, SDEs, and shared crossings invites many perspectives and possible interpretations. What they have in common are shifts in states of consciousness. Changes in levels of consciousness can be observed and measured in the dying. For loved ones or caregivers, perhaps the shift is one of awareness—a quality of presence that allows an opening to the dying person's experience.

Like a jewel-cut prism, experience and the meaning ascribed to it will be shaped by focus—by which facets the light strikes and is reflected back to the observer.

THE SHARED CROSSING

I have come to understand the shared crossing with my mother as a journey that began long before the end of her life. Our journey has been a lengthy one—at times, arduous, tedious, exhausting, and painful, yet also funny, ultimately poignant, fulfilling, and a labor of love.

I will start with a plea for forgiveness. As inconvenient as it may be for the scholars, I will let go of any formal definition of shared crossings in order to tell my story. *Passages* or *Shared Journey* might serve just as well, but the rebel in me clings to the title *Shared Crossing*. It serves my purpose to shift the focus away from terms or categorization—and onto the process.

To the best of my ability, this story is true to my experience. Like any long journey, the voyage leaves some memories forgotten, with details and the exact order of things blurred like a mirage in the desert.

In the Beginning ...

Perhaps the shared crossing with my mother begins at birth, but have mercy on the reader; for my purposes, I need not begin there.

My mother moved from Austin, Texas, to Santa Barbara in the autumn of 2008 "to be closer to [her] daughters." My parents had separated the summer I graduated from high school, and Mom's long-term partner moved east to be cared for by his family. I lived and worked in Santa Barbara, and my older sister, Carolyn, was in the San Francisco area. Our younger sister, Ruth, lived across the country in New York. The majority wins—or perhaps the charms of Santa Barbara, despite my mother's strong ties to the east.

At the age of 79, Mom was spry, active, and sociable. I was divorced, happily single, and enjoyed time with friends and the great outdoors. I don't like "exercise," but I love to hike up a hillside and take in a view of the ocean. For me, going to the gym meant dance classes and regular practice of yoga and tai chi. Those activities became the ballast that kept my ship afloat during challenging times.

Over the years, I'd worked in social services, business administration, the entertainment industry, and education. When Mom arrived, I was establishing my career in psychology as a faculty member at the graduate school where I'd earned my doctorate. At the time of Mom's move, my mother and I had not lived in the same city, or even the same state, for more than thirty years. Still, Mom was the center knot that kept the family together.

My sisters flew to Texas and packed Mom's home into the back of a moving van while I awaited the renovation of an apartment I'd found for her in Santa Barbara. Carolyn would drive Mom from Austin to California, where she would begin the new and final chapter of her life.

This is where our story began to turn—of us taking care of Mom instead of Mom taking care of us—although that certainly would not have been her experience. My mother's identity was of being ferociously capable and independent. In truth, she would be able to live on her own until the summer of 2017.

In the fall of 2009, my mother was diagnosed with colon cancer. She greeted the news with courage, or more aptly, in a matter-of-fact manner. "No big deal." She had survived surgery and radiation treatment for endometrial cancer in 1997. She was confident that this was just another bump in the road and that she would recover. With some tender care from her oncologist and her daughters— she did.

My Mother, the Wild Woman ...

I was a young child when our family—Mom, Dad, and three girls—moved into our home in Belle Isle, South Carolina. Belle Isle was a housing development that hadn't happened yet. The backyard behind our red brick house sloped down to a lake that was more of a swamp. Trees grew out of the water, with some masking duck-hunting blinds. In other places, cypress trees and their knobby knees protruded from its murky waters. I remember our family canoeing on that lake, our boxer dog, Brunie, swimming alongside. That felt terribly dangerous in a lake populated with alligators, their eyes raised just above the surface, hiding their torsos and muscled tails.

I was about five when the phone rang, and Mom got the call. One of our closest neighbors had an alligator in her driveway. "Martha," she cried, "I can't get the car out of the garage to get to a doctor's appointment!" Dad was at work, so Mom packed three kids into the back of the car and drove down the road to a friend in distress. This is a true story—I know ... I was there. Mom got out of the car to consider her options. We stood nearby and watched as she lassoed the alligator with a nylon rope and tied it to the front bumper of the car. She then backed down the dirt road all the way home ... dragging the alligator through the dust.

As it turned out, the man working on our air conditioner had been an alligator wrestler. He shot the beast my mother had wrangled, and then he dressed the meat for dinner. As abhorrent as this may seem to those concerned about animal cruelty, this is how it was—back in the woods, back in the day—and these were the skills of a woman raised in the hills of Pennsylvania. Even now, a tingle runs down my spine with memories of a place where a thin veneer of Southern gentility covered the wildness of nature.

My mother had a certain bravado when it came to nature. I was about six when our family moved from South Carolina to Champaign, Illinois, where my father had been offered work as a research assistant and professor in the

Department of Forestry. Within a week of our arrival, our family cat was ripped open by a neighborhood dog. Flapping skin exposed the smooth surface of the belly below. This event was met with the same boldness as the alligator. After a trip to the drug store to purchase chloroform, Mom put the cat to sleep and sewed up the torn side with a needle and thread. That cat would go on to have several litters of kittens.

Mom's knack for wrangling the wild continued at my high school. After she earned a Master's degree in English in Illinois, our family moved to Madison, Wisconsin, where my father would complete his Ph.D. in Land Resource Economics. There my mother taught two English classes for a year at West High—one for problem students. Twenty-eight "bad boys" and two girls were tamed by passing around a live boa constrictor for a writing assignment.

Mother. Emlenton, PA. Age six.

My mother grew up in the hills of Pennsylvania, wading the creeks and roaming the countryside, bow and arrow in hand. Sometimes with other children. Often alone.

I don't know when my mother lost her more adventurous and creative sides. Or where I lost my own. Perhaps it is the cost of maturity—the responsibilities that come with being a mother, making a living, or making it on our own. Growing up requires a loss of innocence, and sometimes, a loss of play.

Perhaps it is the nature of things ...
Losing and finding. Losing and finding ...
Parts of ourselves ...
Again and again.

Or ... perhaps adventure and creativity are
shapeshifters ...
Taking on different forms over time ...
In a search to become whole.

———

The Landscape Begins to Change ...

My mother recovered from the cancer diagnosed in 2009, but by 2014 I was already concerned about her memory and self-sufficiency in the long run. I began seeding the possibility of her moving to an independent living community directly across the street. I believed more activities and companionship would improve her quality of life. It would also take some of the pressure off of me. We already shared custody of my cat because both Mom and my cat needed more attention than I could give. A move? Mom would have none of it! She enjoyed being in her apartment complex among people of all ages, especially families with young children that formed special bonds with her. Like many seniors, she did not identify with being older. *She did not like "old people!"*

This was where self-concept and reality began to collide. My mother had always been a highly capable and resourceful person who had much to give. She'd volunteered at Mendota State Mental Hospital in Madison, Wisconsin, when we were children, then taught the most difficult students at my high school when I was a teen. She returned to graduate school at the age of 50 and earned a Master's degree in Counseling at Gallaudet University in Washington, D.C. She was among the minority of hearing students at a college for the hearing impaired. I was in my late 20s when I traveled down from New York for a weekend visit. I found my mother in a new and quiet land, vibrant and animated with the language of sound and movement. Hands flew in the dining hall. Bellows and murmurs echoed through the halls of Mom's dorm room that night.

My mother had learned sign language and moved to Austin, Texas, to begin a career working with children and families. She held a unique specialty that enabled her to serve the deaf community. In Santa Barbara, she now filled her life with gardening and forming relationships with her neighbors. Mom felt that she had retired too soon.

A Downward Spiral ...

After a lengthy process, at the end of 2014, my mother was finally approved to work at the YMCA as a volunteer in their daycare program. She was now 85. Mom was beloved by the kids, and her talents were recognized by the staff. Unfortunately, this signaled the beginning of a downward slide. Daycares and sticky-handed children, with all their clinging affections, are also the breeding ground for germs. Almost immediately, she became seriously ill with respiratory problems and needed to take a leave of absence. After several tries, it became clear that she could not return. She struggled to remain involved by attempting to design a curriculum that would improve their programs. Her desire was strong, but the ideas remained actions that could not be carried through. Signs of her cognitive decline were showing.

2015: THE YEAR OF MOM

Our lives took a dramatic turn in 2015. It would mark the beginning of my three-year role as a caregiver. Taking care of an aging parent is a practice in patience—a lesson that I would have to learn, time and time again.

Following my mother's close encounters with small children, she had bouts of pneumonia and bronchiectasis four times in the first six months of 2015. This involved numerous urgent care visits, followed by trips to her doctor.

A Mystery Unfolds ...

While I was working to establish my practice at the Family Therapy Institute as a licensed psychotherapist, I also needed to solve the mystery of what was happening with Mom. When she was not feeling well, she was argumentative. She would insist on a brand of nutritional supplements from a specific store that—despite my best efforts as the good and dutiful daughter—I could not find. When she was ill, she literally lost her mind and could not be trusted with the simplest of tasks. I would carefully organize her supplements and prescriptions into the morning and evening compartments of her pill dispenser. She would insist that she had taken her medication though it was still in its designated box. It became clear that the days of the week had little meaning to her. Pills moved around the boxes, and a stray might be found next to a decaying chunk of food on the floor.

My mother was on her umpteenth visit to the urgent care clinic, directly next to her apartment complex, when I got a call at my office. Mom had walked the short distance across the parking lot to the clinic many times before. I usually went with her to follow-up visits or took her to her primary physician for continued care. This time she needed to be picked up and accompanied home.

When I arrived, a nurse took me to the room where my mother balanced on the edge of an examination table, her thin limbs dangling from beneath a hospital gown. I wrapped a blanket around her shoulders while we waited for the doctor to arrive with instructions and prescriptions. After he left, I helped Mom pull a pale-yellow turtleneck over her tattered bra. Her drooping tissue looked more like empty satchels than breasts. I'd tried to buy her something better, but nothing was as comfortable as the tried and true.

I knew that taking antibiotics *as prescribed* was essential for her recovery. As we prepared to leave, I began to explain that I would hold her medications and deliver them to her twice a day. When she insisted that she could do it herself, I blurted, "No, Mom. You are going to do exactly what I tell you to do … When you are sick, you have no mind!" The sharpness in my voice surprised us both. She stared back at me wide-eyed as my frustration dissolved into tears. "This is hard for me, too," I said.

Thus began our routine. I delivered medications twice a day and pressed each pill into the palm of her hand. I watched as she put it into her mouth and swallowed. She accepted this reluctantly at first, sticking out her tongue at me like an angry child.

My mother's thinking and behavior fluctuated with her health. I knew from a colleague that the elderly can be derailed by something as simple as dehydration or a urinary tract infection—but was there something more?

April 17, 2015. Ironically, or divinely ordained, it was on my birthday that I took my mother to her first appointment with a neurologist who specializes in dementia. Mom and I sat across a large desk from Dr. Harbaugh. His warm and easy-going manner seemed to lighten the seriousness of why we were there. I needed answers.

In that first meeting, I noticed Mom did not respond directly to Dr. Harbaugh's questions. Instead, she told him much about her life and her accomplishments. As I listened, I thought, *"She wants him to know that she's not just some little old lady who's sick."* It is only now that I realize she may not have understood the questions or could not hold them in her mind long enough to respond.

While Dr. Harbaugh engaged Mom in conversation, he jotted brief notes that provided clues to what he was seeing. In the future, he continued to pass notes to me at the end of our meetings. Dr. Harbaugh gave Mom the gift of recognizing her intelligence—feeling important, seen, and heard. This provided her with a sense of capability and control. There would be no resistance to seeing Dr. Harbaugh.

It was not the birthday I would have planned, but as presents go, it was a good one. Happy birthday to me!

A battery of psychological tests and an MRI followed. The scans showed no signs of stroke or tumors. However, the psych testing showed Mom's short-term memory was in the first to second percentile. You really can't get much worse than that. It was not until much later that I could fully appreciate how well she managed to function over the next two years.

The pieces of the puzzle were beginning to fit. In our follow-up meeting, Dr. Harbaugh diagnosed mild cognitive impairment (MCI)—a likely precursor to Alzheimer's. The impairment did not feel very mild to me. The note he pushed across the desk that day said, "Three to six years." I understood that to mean her life expectancy.

The brain sends important messages to the body, and both of hers were breaking down. Fortunately, pneumonia and bronchiectasis had put other practical matters in place earlier in the year. Mom's physician had prescribed assisted home health visits by a nurse, as well as physical and occupational therapy to support her recovery. We had also met with a social worker who provided resource information and recommended that I obtain durable power of attorney. As "the boots on the ground," I became the primary person responsible for my mother's health and financial decisions. My name went on her bank account so I could pay her rent and bills. I had already participated in meetings with her financial advisor for some time. In those meetings, Mom smiled and chatted about her life while I did my best to understand the recommendations and okay the plans.

During Mom's various illnesses, I researched and tried meal delivery programs, picked up groceries, and administered medications. I apprised my sisters of all developments in detail, which served to organize me as much as to inform them. I met with a counselor at the Alzheimer's Association several times alone and then later with my sisters in attendance. All three of us needed to understand what was happening so that we could work together as a team. For every detail I have shared, there would be hundreds more. This is what it meant to be my mother's daughter—and now her primary caregiver.

One does not fully understand the importance of details and preparation until the next crisis comes. We had begun to solve the mystery of Mom's shifting capacities when a bout of pneumonia put her in the hospital that June. My sisters and I began to examine her long-term care policy and research housing options. Still optimistic, I put Mom's name on the list at the independent living facility she had rejected earlier. When Ruth visited, we looked at assisted living facilities for when Mom would need more. The shock of the costs, and the condition of residents in assisted living, was a glimpse of what the future might look like—a sobering experience that I am grateful to have not faced alone. Remarkably, with all of that in place, Mom did recover. She was able to return to her apartment and community of neighbors.

In the fall of 2015, Mom and I worked through her anxiety so that she could fly to New York, where both my sisters now lived. I was desperate for her to go. I needed a break! All of Mom's fears revolved around the weather and potential disasters. With a wing and a prayer for no major events in the Western hemisphere, good planning, and wheelchair assists at every stop, Mom was able to make the trip alone. After a month in New York, she returned energized and more confident.

2015 was a year of increased and ongoing responsibilities that I called Project Mom.

When I was a child, I watched the 1966 TV series Mission Impossible on our boxy black-and-white television. Every week a team of secret agents was given a tape-recorded message with only the most hazardous of assignments. Each member brought with them their own special expertise. Of course, I would need to be the intrepid Cinnamon Carter. By 2015, I had been handed a mission that I chose to accept—and it would take a full team to be able to say, "Mission accomplished."

2016: IT WAS
A VERY GOOD YEAR

Notes of the Frank Sinatra tune come to mind. That was her generation. The lyrics crooned by "Ol' Blue Eyes" spoke of a very good year.

2016 Was a Pretty Good Year ...

My mother was ill at least five times in 2015. In 2016, she was sick only once. I had learned from experience that immediate intervention was key. Any sign of her chronic respiratory problems meant a quick call to her doctor and the prescription of strong antibiotics. We both knew the drill. I delivered her medications, and Mom recovered this time without even a trip to the doctor.

I settled into my responsibilities without all the ongoing crises. In February, I organized Mom's tax receipts and delivered them to her accountant for the first time. Mom had been able to do this on her own up until now. In November, Mom reviewed pamphlets for the election, made her choices, and asked to consult with me before returning her mail-in ballot. That was easy. When it comes to politics, we agree! These details may seem insignificant, but they are important. Mom was still able to think, but was giving up her battle for control. She was asking for help and receiving it.

There were pleasures, great and small. We played Scrabble, and Mom, forever the English teacher, could put down obscure words that I needed to confirm by looking them up in the dictionary. Was it really a word? She was usually right. My suspicions were not unfounded, Mom could beat me at Scrabble, but she could not add up the score. For her, two plus two did not always equal four.

During symphony season, we attended lively talks each month at Valle Verde Retirement Center. Mom made a special connection with the presenter, Ramon Araiza, who sat at a grand piano and told colorful stories about the composers and their times. Mom loved Ramon, part music historian and part comedian, and he loved her back. At the end of each talk, Mom went up to give him compliments, and he gave her hugs. Ramon is a national treasure and came to feel like a friend. We shared a special understanding. He, too, was taking care of his aging mother.

Mom was still able to drive the simple route to Trader Joe's to pick up groceries, encounter friends, or strike up a conversation in the vegetable aisle. She continued to participate in activities in her philanthropic women's group once or twice a month and attended services at Unity Church. Occasionally she visited the YMCA to look in on the children she'd so hoped to work with. Some of the children still remembered her, and this gave her great joy.

My mother's greatest pleasure was the Hispanic couple that moved in next door and adopted her as a member of their extended family. She followed the pregnancy and birth of their first child, Luna. She was treated as a grandmother—included in the inner circle at Luna's christening and the celebration that followed. What a gift this family was to her.

Along with the bright spots, there were the blind spots. Mine.

Mom was incredibly resourceful. Post-it notes with phone numbers and things she wanted to remember were scattered around her apartment. She kept a notebook to track what she did each day so that she could hold a conversation during our evening calls. These conversations could be excruciatingly boring as she reported in exact detail what she had eaten that day. This was a ritual held over from 2015 when she became so thin it seemed like the next illness might blow her away like a feather on the wind.

At the time, I did not fully understand that habits, familiarity, and routine are the saving grace for people with memory loss. I tried to listen patiently and developed a list of questions that might keep things more interesting. "How did that go?" "What did you enjoy today?" "Did the mailman feed the crows?" I also had a pocket full of exit lines. "I've had a long day at the office; I need to make dinner now." Mom could talk endlessly if given the chance.

Life can be desperately lonely when time bends and does not fit neatly into a twenty-four-hour day. My sisters coordinated their calls from New York, and Mom might speak to one of them during the day—but not remember that night. I longed for Mom to live in a community where she would have daily activities and social interactions that did not depend on me.

Our final meeting with Dr. Harbaugh was in June, just before his retirement. He did not seem concerned that Mom was still living alone or driving short distances to familiar places. Short-term memory can be impaired, while long-term memory and driving skills are not. In truth, most of the bumps and scratches on the car belonged to me. With no marked changes in Mom's condition, we did not seek another neurologist. Previous meetings and information from the Alzheimer's Association provided support.

D. A. R. E.

D. A. R. E. is an essential acronym from the Alzheimer's Association:

<u>D</u>o not

   <u>A</u>rgue

      <u>R</u>eason or

         <u>E</u>xplain.

To do otherwise was pointless. Mom was unlikely to remember what was said—by her or by me. The simple wisdom of D.A.R.E. conserved energy and prepared the ground for another strategy that kept me sane.

Seed the Positive ...

With dementia, it is no longer about what someone thinks or whether or not it is true—*It is about how they feel*. I learned to keep seeding the positive ... strategically timed and not all at once. "Wouldn't it be nice to eat dinner with other people every day?" At another time, "This independent and assisted living place has really great activities to choose from ... The Friendship Center has programs that could support your memory and help keep you healthy ..." Creating good feelings and my enthusiasm were the path through this strange and unpredictable land.

My sisters and I understood the stages of Alzheimer's disease from consultation with and written materials from the Alzheimer's Association. Applying that knowledge was a different matter. There is a natural inclination to want to keep our loved ones happy, but the looming question was not, "Is she happy?" but "Is she safe?"

Living in Limbo ...

"Is she safe?" It seemed like such a simple question—with no simple black-and-white answer. A large expanse of gray seemed to spread out before me that I did not know how to cross. My mother's diagnosis was mild cognitive impairment, not Alzheimer's. Mom was still managing on her own—and she did not like change. She did not want to move!

I lived in constant uncertainty. What was the right thing to do? There comes a time when the adult children of aging parents must take control and become the decision-makers to ensure their safety—but when is that?

It is difficult to understand what the loss of short-term memory meant for my mother and for me. It happened in fits and starts, and it happened over time. I began to notice when we watched a movie together that Mom had difficulty following the storyline. Her memory could not hold from scene to scene. Family visits were exciting and much anticipated, but Mom seemed lost in any conversation that involved more than one other person.

There came a day when I began to understand. Both my sisters were visiting from New York, and we were sitting at the dining room table after a lovely meal **that Carolyn had prepared.** Without getting up from the table, Mom repeated the same story twice. Furthermore, what she shared seemed unrelated to what we were talking about—a pause in the conversation simply signaled a time for her to speak. For her, those two moments were not connected in time. There was only one moment for Mom—the "now." I glanced over at Ruth. Was she getting this? A flash of recognition passed between us.

Just as a parent does not notice the changes happening in their child from day to day—I don't remember exactly when or how it happened—but Mom's life was becoming smaller. Over the course of the year, Mom's movement slowed and everything seemed to take more effort. Time spent in her garden faded away. She stopped participating in her women's group or going to church. She could no longer remember how to make the beef stew she'd made for decades. Instead, she drove the half block to Whole Foods to piece together her meals from the buffet.

There were still glimmers of light. Brief interactions

with baby Luna in the arms of mom or dad were still her gold.

In October, plans were made for Mom to spend two weeks with my sisters in New York. I felt they needed more time to understand what was really happening, but I would take what I could get. I was bending under the weight of responsibility. I needed our mother to be in a place where others' eyes would be on her every day. That was not going to happen unless the three of us seeded a clear and consistent message. Fortunately, before Mom left for New York, she agreed to participate in a group once a week at the Friendship Center upon her return. It was a start.

The Friendship Center is designed for people with memory loss and offers classes, groups, and daycare services. My mother was not yet at the stage to need full-day care, but the road was headed in that direction.

At the airport, I stood vigilant outside the window as Mom passed through security, armed with written instructions and phone numbers to present if anything went wrong. I watched as she placed her purse, jacket, and lunch on the conveyor belt. My heart sank when she did not recognize her belongings at the other end. She stood there helpless and confused until airline personnel sorted her and led her to her gate. I left with a knot in my stomach. What had I done?

The image of my mother looking like a forlorn child was seared into my brain. I was only six years old when our family moved from the woods in South Carolina to a city in Illinois. On my first day of elementary school, I was fascinated by a girl in my class with tight curls framing her face that looked like a helmet to me. Sally had the "bubble perm," all the rage in the city back in the day. I also heard the "Grand Canyon Suite" for the first time, sparking my love for classical music and visions of red canyon walls and the rocky slopes leading down to the river. Maybe I was supposed to wait for my sister ... but as I walked home on my own that day, I studied my feet, imagining the clip-clop of burro hooves as they made their way down the trail. I looked up to find the straight lines of sidewalks in a sub-urban neighborhood, with ranch-style homes and neatly clipped lawns that I did not recognize; I then stood on a front porch and rang the doorbell of a woman I did not know. She called my mother. Now, I imagined my mother in a huge airport, with hundreds of people filing by—lost, like I had been—a stranger in a strange land.

Despite my guilt for having allowed my mother to travel alone, she made it to New York and back and had a won-derful time. In November, she began attending a group at Friendship Center once, then twice a week. My fears had not vanished. I insisted that she accept services from Easy Lift and arranged door-to-door transportation. Driving the half block to Whole Foods or the familiar route to Trader Joe's was one thing. Driving the distance to Friendship Center was another.

As a whole, Mom enjoyed the Friendship Center, though she repeated complaints about one of the women in the group over and over again. True to form, she had lots of ideas about how the program could be improved. With or without complaints, the weight on my shoulders became a little lighter.

At times, living in limbo felt like being stretched across the sea—with fear on one shore and hope on the other. Although my mother's cognitive capacities were declining, our relationship was growing and continued to change. Mom was becoming warmer, more appreciative, and willing to listen. I was learning to listen more deeply. Her heart was opening, and opening mine.

In 2016, I assisted in two workshops offered by the Shared Crossing Project that expanded my picture of what was needed for this journey. I was not without a map ... but I could not know how long the trip, or the direction it might take. Philosophically, neither my mother nor I were afraid of death—but the path forward would not be an easy one.

2017: THE LONG ROAD "HOME"

New Territory ...

The strands that kept my mother tied to her community were loosening. She'd formed special relationships with the children in her apartment complex, which were welcomed by their parents. The Chinese family with two young boys moved to Oklahoma. Special dishes would no longer arrive unexpectedly at her door, and she would not be able to bake them apple pies. Other neighbors who had stopped to chat on the now rare occasions she was in her garden were gone. The family next door that had adopted her as a grandmother to baby Luna bought a home. Now it was furniture, not a babe in arms, that made its way past her window and down the stairs. Mom was finally ready to consider a move.

The year before, I had identified an independent and assisted living facility that I thought might meet the least resistance. Wood Glen Hall is a lovely and astonishingly affordable residence only ten minutes from my apartment. I had been warned against looking at places at a distance, where the best of intentions can give way to the practicalities of time and effort. I had visited a number of facilities, and the comfortable, friendly atmosphere at Wood Glen Hall seemed like a fit—fancy and formal were not for Mom. Wood Glen Hall offered large, well-lit areas where people could gather to socialize and a rich schedule of activities and performances. There were craft rooms, game rooms, a library, and even a place to meditate. In the main dining room, she would be able to share meals with people who would become familiar—and, with time, friends.

I did not imagine downsizing Mom from her spacious two-bedroom, two-bath apartment with a view of the mountains into a single room and bath would be easy. Still, I was hopeful. Wood Glen Hall sits at the bottom of a hill where chaparral and palms stretch up behind. Ample walkways surrounded the perimeter, and beautiful garden courtyards were at the center of each wing. I envisioned Mom tending her own small garden along with others. Above all, it was now nature that made Mom happy.

My bucolic vision of what was possible came to a sudden halt when my sister Carolyn decided she wanted Mom to move to New York. I had been working towards a plan for several years. Had the many hours of effort been wasted? Some older sister/younger sister dynamics came into play. Did she think I was not doing a good enough job? I imagined Carolyn had a romanticized view of what it meant to take care of our mother. They had pleasant times and fun activities when Mom visited for several weeks, but that was far removed from the reality—daily calls, trips to the doctor—her neurologist, eye doctor, dermatologist, hearing aid tests and fittings, annual mammogram, home healthcare workers, social workers—then meetings with her financial planner, the bank, her accountant, and an attorney ... Did she think she could do it better?

My younger sister Ruth was focused on pragmatics and asked a very good question, "What do you think would be best for you and for Mom?" The question stopped me in my tracks. I had been doing what needed to be done for so long that I rarely stopped to think about what might be best for me. Maybe Carolyn could do it better. I was exhausted, and she wanted the job. I was ready to pass the baton.

I began to let go. New York might be the right place for our mother at the end of her life. She grew up in Pennsylvania, and that was the landscape in her bones. There were more activities there Mom could participate in—Carolyn's wool spinning group (Mom loved to pick debris from the raw fleece and card the newly spun yarn), local festivals, her husband's music concerts, weekends in their home, drives to see the autumn colors, and shared family holidays. There would be more "boots on the ground"— two daughters instead of one. We needed to consider the options.

Along with relief came a sense of fear and loss. Mom's life had become smaller, and so had mine. I had been so caught up in my work with clients and the demands of caregiving that I had little energy to tend to my own life and relationships. What would life be like without her?

I would have to rebuild.

When my mother arrived in Santa Barbara, we had not lived in proximity for many years. During our time together, I'd learned much about my mother—and about myself. The woman who moved to Santa Barbara in 2008 was no longer the mother who raised me as a child. Our relationship had evolved, and some of the inevitable wounds of childhood had healed. Perhaps my sisters needed to have their own experiences with our mother at this stage of life.

May 14, 2017, Mother's Day. Before I headed over to Mom's apartment with her favorite lunch and carrot cake from Natural Cafe, I got a call from Ruth. I was stunned by the news. Ruth had spoken with Mom that morning, and Mom was asking to move up the visit to Wood Glen Hall. I was ecstatic—not so much about visiting Wood Glen Hall, but the fact that Mom was initiating the conversation! I proceeded with caution when it came to the subject of a move. Mom never said it to me directly, but I had not forgotten that she'd told Ruth that I was "trying to put her away." Now confidence was building that a move might actually happen.

Ruth and Carolyn looked at places in New York the following week and found a viable option not far from Carolyn's work. I knew it was a good place—it was part of a chain, virtually a duplicate of one I had seen here in California when visiting a friend. It operated under the same model—

size, floor plans, and social activities. Located in upstate New York, Mom could afford a one-bedroom apartment instead of one room in Santa Barbara. It lacked the hominess of Wood Glen Hall, but more space for familiar belongings and the availability of family balanced the scales. Mom could decide what was best for her.

We were fortunate that Mom was still capable of participating in the process. However, I suspected it would not be a reasoned comparison or a clear choice. With her memory issues, Mom lived very much in the moment. If she liked wherever she was, she would likely say yes—to both. It would be up to her daughters to sway the decision. I needed to make peace with whichever way it went.

On May 25, Mom and I toured the grounds, the available rooms, and the amenities at Wood Glen Hall. Mom loved it! After a chair yoga class and lunch in the dining room—where she enjoyed the food and the attention of gentlemen at the next table—we met with the director. After battling a move for so long, Mom said her only regret was that she hadn't done it sooner. Surprise and relief came with a dagger to my heart—for how all my efforts had been twisted in the past, and at the same time, a sense of failure for not having made it happen.

We began the paperwork for admittance, doctor's clearance, and facility approval. We put down a deposit with a move-in date scheduled for July 1. There would be no pushback from my sisters.

A Change of Plans ...

At the beginning of June, I was preparing for the move—some of which I did surreptitiously. I was careful to preserve a sense of order, fearing that Mom might change her mind. My sisters would arrive closer to the move-in date to help sort, distribute, and organize the estate sale. I knew that any change was difficult for Mom. It now seemed almost too good to be true that her willingness and the move to Wood Glen Hall were happening so quickly.

June 7, 2017. I was at my mother's apartment almost daily when I noticed that she was becoming lethargic. She complained of pain in one shoulder that, in the past, had been a precursor to pneumonia. She did not have a fever, but I took her to the doctor as a preventative measure. It seemed an inopportune moment for her to become ill with the impending move only three weeks away. I was determined for her to be well and ready—as if my own survival depended on it. Her physician detected a crackle in her lungs and diagnosed pleurisy, an inflammation of the lung tissue. Prescription in hand, I was not terribly concerned—I had done this before. I began the daily medication and food deliveries while continuing my efforts toward the move. My routine of caring for Mom was interspersed with time at my office. It felt like just another turn on the merry-go-round.

June 10. This time was different. After more than two full days on antibiotics, my mother was running a low fever. I feared that pleurisy might be turning into pneumonia and another trip to the hospital. It seemed that the best-laid plans for the move might evaporate. It was a Saturday when I tried to reach her doctor on his on-call line. I busied myself cleaning Mom's kitchen and other household tasks while awaiting a return call. After an hour and a half, I gave up and returned to my apartment to retrieve an oral thermometer after getting inconsistent readings on the one Mom had. I was mortified to discover that, in my panic, I'd left my home phone number on the on-call line—instead of my cell phone or Mom's landline. I now had two irritated messages from her doctor.

I rushed back to my mother's apartment to take her temperature and call back with accurate information—and to explain and apologize. From my description of Mom's symptoms, her doctor did not think she needed to be hospitalized. She was not having trouble breathing, she could keep food down, and he said that it was not unusual for a fever to spike under treatment with antibiotics. He instructed me to give her Tylenol for fever and comfort and to keep an eye on her. By the time I left, Mom had no fever and was feeling better. She was comfortably seated in front of the television for her evening shows.

Twists and Turns. Bits and Pieces ...

June 11. Morning, noon, and night. Life is full of surprises. When I arrived the next morning, Mom was still sitting in her chair, a bit confused but in bright spirits. She was aware that she had been there all night but told me that she had been at a party! I knew from past experience that when Mom was ill, her mind could be loopy. From my studies and participation in the Shared Crossing work-shops, I also knew that people towards the end of life can have fascinating experiences.

I met the news of the party with curiosity. Was this a delusion or what is called a *pre-death vision*? It didn't really matter—I knew that it was meaningful. "Who was at the party?" I asked. She wasn't able to say but asked the name of my boyfriend.

"He was there," she said. This was good news! I didn't have a boyfriend, but perhaps he was on his way! I thought of Michael. I call him "my most loved person in the uni-verse" because he is no longer in this world. It is Michael who taught me about unconditional love.

I made breakfast, and when we sat down to eat, Mom seemed more lucid—able to separate her experience from reality. Or so I thought. She then asked if the party I was planning was that afternoon. Still planting seeds for the move, I said, "No, there is no party this afternoon. You might be thinking about the party we will have at Wood Glen Hall when you start a new, fun chapter of your life."

I waited awhile before asking again about the party. She ate very slowly. She was clearly in an altered state and spoke haltingly, with long pauses amid fragments of thought. Between bites of oatmeal and meds, bit by bit, she began to describe parts of her experience. "It was as if I could see all the things that I have done in my life. The good things, and the things I wish I hadn't done ... It was as if I could reach out and touch the pictures and all the colors."

Was she in the midst of a life review that comes at life's end? She seemed without judgment—there was a sense of wholeness and calm.

As I listened to her experience, I breathed it into my body. The tension and pain I had been carrying in my right shoulder for several months lessened. The room felt lighter and more spacious. Some might say that guardian angels or guides were present. If so, I couldn't see them.

Mom then said, "I think I'll be around a bit longer ..."

This was a change. Mom always spoke as if she expected to live a long life—like her mother, who died at the age of 101. I hung suspended in the threads of uncertainty of what all of this might mean.

What I did know was that we were in transition. The veil between life and death was very thin.

In that moment, my mother seemed at peace with it. And so was I.

My sister, Carolyn, called that day to say she was trying to arrange to come out and help. I took a deep, grateful breath. It felt important to have Carolyn there for whatever might come next—support for Mom's recovery, the move to Wood Glen Hall, a convalescent home, or the end of life.

I felt calm and enthralled in these conversations with my mother. What Mom described was consistent with what

I knew about shared crossings. However, somewhere during that day, the tides began to change. Mom could no longer move on her own and needed help getting up from the table to move to her chair, from the chair to the bathroom, and back.

It is one thing to be philosophical about death and quite another to be faced with the reality that she might actually be dying. I was in turmoil about whether to call an ambulance that would take her to the hospital, to be poked and prodded and perhaps brought halfway back to life. I knew most people prefer to die at home, though very few do. In the past, my mother told me that she would prefer to die if she could not recover to a better life. She'd said point blank, "If I can't take care of myself, I want to go to hospice and die." Still, I was uncertain about what was actually happening—and there were others involved. If Carolyn knew how dire things looked, would she want Mom taken to the hospital so that she could see her before she was gone?

I called both my sisters. Carolyn felt that she'd already had the conversations and shared the memories she need-ed to with Mom. We agreed that keeping Mom at home was the best answer for now. Carolyn would get on a plane the next day. I called Ruth to share our thoughts. We were all on the same page.

Later that evening, Mom was even weaker. She had no fever but said that she was cold. She did not seem in pain and was not having trouble breathing. As I left, she was curled on the couch with her favorite stuffed animal under her arm, a scraggly lion that she'd bought at a thrift store.

There was a faint smile on her face.

I was in torment—but I could not stay. Mom kept her apartment at what, for me, was an unbearably hot temperature. In truth, I was suffocating under the agony and fear of not making the right decisions.

June 12, 6:30 AM. With a mind left in turmoil, I had not slept a wink. As my hand turned on the doorknob, it held the shame of not sitting by my mother's side through the night. I expected to find her lifeless. Instead, the woman who could not move on her own the night before was now perched on the edge of the couch—her eyes clear. I felt a mix of confusion and relief. I had not failed entirely and would have another chance.

I had canceled all my clients for the day and resumed my caregiving routine—food, meds, and organizing the apartment. I picked up the Physicians Orders for Life Sustaining Treatment (POLST) from Mom's doctor's office that she had signed in 2015. A POLST is completed when a person is competent, clarifies their wishes, and serves as instruction to their doctor when they are no longer able to do so. I would be prepared for anything. A POLST was also required for new residents before admission to Wood Glen Hall. With a mind deprived of sleep, I lived in hope that the move would still happen. I did what I could. I kept taking one step after another ...

At lunch, Mom was caught again within her own musings ... slumped at the table, eyes closed between slow bites of food. I let go of prompting her to eat and wondered what she might be seeing. I decided to try and enter her world and asked what she remembered about her own mother at the end of her life. This roused her out of her trance and into engagement.

"Something came up ... some kind of illness ... When she [her mother] was in the hospital, she was lying there and talking like I am talking to you now ... and then 'he' came and took a bite out of her."

"Who is he?" I asked.

"I don't know ... something dark. Something they didn't like very much."

"Who are they?"

"The family," she replied.

Brow furled, she was clearly grappling with my questions and her own thoughts. She made small movements with her hands and fingers. There was something she was trying to work out as she said, "... It's folded up like a piece of paper ... between the past and the future."

"... It is unfolding," I said quietly.

"It's good to be able to think about these things without it bothering me," she replied. "There should be a circle of people who help others with their memories ... and help them clear their minds."

Was she referring to clearing shame and self-recrimination? Regrets? I understood her to mean that there should be people to help with suffering—to understand their lives in the way that she was understanding hers in that moment.

Wondering if she was in a different otherworldly realm, I said, "You've done that in your life ... maybe you are becoming one of the people in that circle."

Her tone was reflective and serene, though she says, "I feel like my life is going in a circle and I have stayed too long ... If I get better, I want to ..." Her voice drifted off until she asked, "Are you going to call the people you call when people are saying these kinds of crazy things?"

"No. I don't think it's crazy. People talk about these kinds of things towards the end of their lives."

She pointed and asked, "Can you see the black curve, like a small black garter snake?"

"No," I answered. "I can't see it, but that doesn't mean it's not there ... You're not really here."

She pointed upwards towards a corner in the ceiling. "There is a little girl there and a small door that is open ... The little girl peeked out the door ... but she didn't touch it."

Later, as Mom sat at the table, not eating, I asked what she was thinking.

"I am thinking about what I want to do when I get home ..."

These exchanges were in keeping with what I knew about shared crossings. "Home" is a theme that appears often in end-of-life conversations.

Throughout the day, Mom moved in and out of different states of energy and awareness. When Carolyn arrived that evening, Mom perked up to receive all the hugs and cuddling she so needed.

No Longer Alone.

Over the next few days, Carolyn took over the care and feeding of Mom while I researched estate and consignment companies. I also tried to identify more options than Wood Glen Hall if Mom's health did not significantly improve.

Carolyn had now joined me in the land of limbo. She observed Mom in a zombie-like state in the morning, then saw her rally for a call I had arranged with Mom's financial planner—a top-rated consultant in the state of Texas—who had served Mom well and felt like a friend. I had informed her of Mom's condition, knowing that she would want to connect before Mom died. During the call, Mom was lucid, chatty, and enthusiastic about the move to Wood Glen Hall. One would never have guessed the ins and outs of her true state.

Carolyn and I kept in close contact with our younger sister, Ruth, still in New York, through daily journals. Carolyn noted this about that day:

"The benefits of moving to Wood Glen Hall are well rehearsed through many tellings—so known territory—while trying to express a thought or describe something she's seeing is not. After lunch, Mom turned back inward, sitting on the couch with her eyes closed most of the afternoon. Then suddenly, around four o'clock, Mom was all there. Damned if I can remember any details of the conversation, but it was a real conversation about the places we find ourselves in our lives. Twenty minutes later, it was back to ... not quite 'word salad,' but I could not figure out what Mom was trying to say."

Mom was eating better, but it would have been a stretch to think she was on the road to recovery. We all agreed it would be helpful to take Mom to her doctor for an assessment.

For the purposes of my story, I have named Mom's doctor "Dr. B." The "B" is for bluster. Like most doctors, he saw too many patients and was always in a hurry. He was an excellent and knowledgeable physician, but spoke at a rate that Mom could never understand. In the past, she would chat with him, forgetting entirely the questions and concerns she had come in with. I had learned to prepare carefully for our meetings with a list of things to be addressed. He was capable of slowing down, listening, and answering questions; however, there was no guarantee that would happen. I was afraid that Mom would rally as she had with her financial planner, and he would not grasp the gravity of the situation.

A Visit to "Dr. B"

Thursday, June 15. I arrived armed with my list—bullet points and all. I was clear about what I wanted to communicate and what I wanted the outcome to be. We needed to review what had happened during the last week, gain his perspective, and find a direction forward. I spoke with the nurse and requested a few minutes alone with the doctor before he saw my mother. Carolyn would sit with her in the waiting room to gain the needed privacy. I was certain Mom would be shocked to hear my report.

Yes, I was prepared. What I was not prepared for was Dr. B when he burst into the room, red-faced, holding his breath, and looking like he was about to explode. The therapist in me stepped forward. "You look really pissed off."

He nodded. "I am."

"Do you want to tell me what that's about?" I asked.

"You are wasting my time! Time I could be examining your mother!"

He went on to list my sins and failures—that I had called him on Saturday and had not been available. He went on, irate, but I couldn't hear him. I had retreated into the depths of my own mind. I was sure that I had apologized profusely, but I did not remind him of that. I felt attacked—I wanted to fight or defend, but my wiser self prevailed. I took a deep breath to calm myself and proceeded to let him know what to expect, that she would rally. I gave my report—quick and dirty. I provided most, but not all of the details I would like to have shared if I felt we could have an actual conversation. As we walked through the door to where my mother was waiting, under my breath, I muttered, "I'm doing the best I can."

In the exam room with my mother, Dr. B softened and proceeded with the assessment. He gave her a Mental Status Exam and reviewed the questions on her POLST. As Dr. B began the process of admitting her to the hospital, I left Carolyn alone in the examining room with Mom. I walked down the hall, past the nurse, and onto the balcony. I broke down and wept.

The soldier that had weathered the attack of Dr. B gave way to the daughter who was trying so desperately to do all the right things. This was not just happening to my mother. This was happening to me. It was happening to us! The family.

I felt the weight of all I had shouldered alone. I was not

alone now. Carolyn was there, and Ruth would arrive that evening.

I felt bludgeoned, but not defeated. We had a path forward.

Shoulder to Shoulder ...

Friday, June 16. Early the next morning, Ruth, Carolyn, and I were at the hospital to ensure we were there before the start of physicians' rounds. Carolyn had witnessed what had happened the day before from the next room. We did not quite know what to expect from Dr. B, but our purpose was clear—to get an update on Mom's condition.

When Dr. B arrived, he looked a little taken aback to find three sisters standing shoulder to shoulder in front of the window. Our mother was laid out on the hospital bed like a giant desk separating us from him. I felt like the center pole, with another placed on either side—as if to hold up a building that might crumble. Emotional exhaustion had taken its toll, but I was surprised to find myself the one speaking. I remember nothing of what was said, only that we gathered the information and, in the end ... I was still standing.

Saturday, June 17. The next morning Carolyn and I arrived at the hospital at about the same time. Ruth stayed at Mom's apartment and dove into the tasks still necessary for a move. "I need to *do something* in order to cope!" she said. We all knew that Mom could not return to her apartment and live alone—regardless of whether or not she recovered.

That morning, I had the sense I needed to have a conversation with my mother, but there were too many disruptions—all the normal activities of a hospital at the beginning of a day. Nurses came and went—there was food to be delivered, vitals to be taken, machines to be monitored, and blood to be drawn. I left for my regular Saturday morning yoga class, leaving Carolyn in Mom's company.

When I returned a few hours later, there was still a flurry of activity. Nurses were trying to adjust the appendage on Mom's arm that kept her IV and monitoring lines in place. When not securely attached, alarms went off and needles gouged her skin. In the midst of all of this, Mom asked a number of times, "Are we going home?" I didn't know if she was speaking of her apartment or another realm that she seemed to visit. If the nurses hadn't been there, I might have said yes.

Later, when the room was quiet, I sat in silence with my mother. Sometimes a smile would cross her face. I wondered, "A memory or a vision?" I had to lean in close to hear her after I asked, "What are you seeing?"

"It's very special to be able to share what I'm seeing with you ..." In the faintest of whispers, haltingly, she began to describe her experience. "There is a place downstairs that is dark ... with entertainment ... or you can entertain yourself ... There is a staircase that goes up ... and a boy ..."

Encouraging her, I responded, "Okay?"

She tried to tell me about a place to put money. At first, I thought she was trying to describe a piggy bank, but that didn't seem right ... An offering plate? Was this boy a gatekeeper? "Pay the piper" before you can advance? Mom was very insistent about the amount of five dollars. "Do you have my checkbook?" she asked.

"No, Mom. Your checkbook is at home, but I have five dollars here ..."

The alarm went off again, and the return of nurses cut our conversation short.

When we were alone again, she spoke about "the boy." "He has blond curly hair ... His eyes are blue."

"Where is she?" I wondered.

"There is a home here, in Santa Barbara, and another home like the place you are seeing in your mind," I said.

"Well then, let's go to Santa Barbara," she replied decisively and upbeat.

A part of me, firmly planted on this earth, wanted to tell her that she would not be going back to her apartment. She would likely be going to a skilled nursing facility. Another part of me wanted to reassure her that there was another home—and that it was okay to go there.

An alarm went off again, and that conversation was not going to happen. Mom winced in pain as the nurses tried to readjust the dressing on her arm once again. After the third or fourth try, I mumbled, "This is just one torture after another."

A young nurse looked at me wide-eyed and asked, "What do you mean?"

Mom had an uncanny way of popping in at just the right moment and said emphatically, "You're hurting me!"

I looked at the nurse and said, "That torture."

When the nurses decided they needed to replace the IV, I had to leave the room. I understood their job, but at that moment, I wasn't sure I understood mine.

When I returned, we were alone again. I'd had enough of the hospital for the day and tried to adjust the bed so that Mom could sleep. That did not go easily. I was struggling to understand how to get her into a more comfortable position when she said, "Any position that will get me in the box!"

She was angry. As I lowered her knees, she said something more about "paying the boy," then snapped, "I'm not going to do this dance! I'm not going to play games with you!" Then, with a tinge of disgust, "I can't believe you are doing all this without the information!"

"Okay, Mom, I'll get your checkbook and pay the boy."

I sat for a moment to regain my composure. There did not seem to be anything I could do to get it right. I wanted to leave, but the voice inside of me kept repeating a phrase I'd heard my whole life, "Don't go away mad." I put on the classical music playlist that I had put together for her—"Winter" from Vivaldi's *Four Seasons*, "The Lark Ascending," "The Flower Duet from Lakme," and Pachelbel's "Canon." I played the music—for both her and for me.

Before I left, I said quietly, "There is a circle of love here. There is a circle of love there. You can go home anytime you want." I moved in closer, "Ruth is here, Carolyn is here, I am here. There is a circle of love, and you can go home anytime."

She nodded, "Okay."

Relief. That night, Ruth, Carolyn, and I went out to dinner at a local joint, Pizza Guru. I laughed to think that a spiritual guru might be just what was needed about now—robes, beard, and all. Pizza, beer, and solidarity with my sisters would have to do.

Later that night, we returned to the hospital together. Avoiding the risk of another failure, I asked the nurse to help my mother get back into bed. Mom was trying to tell me something about "the man with the wires ... it had worked out with the children ... the man you were working with earlier ..." I was trying to make sense of something that did not make sense. That was my fatal flaw.

Mom looked at me again, exasperated.

"I'm just trying to understand," I pleaded.

She snapped back, "Well, it doesn't look like you are understanding!" She had a point there. It's amazing how coherent Mom could be when she was angry. She went on to say, "But I had fun today ..."

My head was spinning. The shared crossing is not all hearts and flowers—or perhaps it is a bed of roses. There will be thorns.

Mom was weak and tired from the trials and tribulations of the day. I was spent. As I prepared to leave, I offered the gentle message that had become a ritual or incantation of sorts—for the first time in front of my sisters. "Your circle of love is here. Ruth is here, Carolyn is here, and I am here ... There is a circle of love here. There is a circle of love there. The circle watches over you while you sleep."

Ruth kissed Mom on the forehead. I kissed my finger-tips and touched them to her hand. We left quietly while Carolyn remained—the curve of her body holding Mom's favorite poetry book created a silhouette against the window. The night sky and lights shimmered beyond.

Expanding the Circle of Love ...

June 18, Father's Day. On Sunday morning, I was exhausted when I headed over to Mom's apartment. Progress needed to be made while Ruth and Carolyn were still there to help. The need to down-size was a certainty—Mom's recovery was not.

It was Father's Day. I might not have remembered except that Ruth and Carolyn were on the phone with Dad and his wife, Judy, when I arrived. After Carolyn and Ruth went back to work, I had the opportunity to speak with my father alone. Although my parents had been divorced for decades, they had maintained a good relationship over the years. My mother had even visited Dad and Judy and stayed at their home in New Bern, North Carolina. Mom lovingly referred to Judy as Dad's "third and final wife." My father turned 95 this year. Thankfully, they have lived up to that moniker. My father was truly interested in Mom's condition and asked, "How are you coping with it all?" Mom's aging and decline only deepened my appreciation for Dad's still-sharp mind and caring conversation.

There was much to accomplish, so Ruth, Carolyn, and I visited Mom in shifts, sometimes separately, sometimes together. I went alone around lunchtime and found Mom in a daze. When I spoke her name, she opened her eyes for only a moment. I learned from the nurse she'd been awake for only about twenty minutes that morning. Mom hadn't eaten anything, but it was unsafe to give her food because she might choke. I asked Mom if she wanted any water. She shook her head no.

I sat in silence, reflecting on my mother's life and the stories she'd told me over time. When she was eleven, her favorite teacher died while mowing his lawn. She'd seen his body lying on the grass. "He looked so peaceful," she'd said. As a young girl, she'd wandered the hills picking flowers for her mother, who was in the hospital with a mysterious illness ...

My grandmother was 40 when my mother was born—quite unusual in 1929. She had been unable to conceive due to an obstruction that was removed with surgery. A successful pregnancy followed, but tragically, my grandmother's first child was strangled at birth by the umbilical cord, which was wrapped around her neck. Baby Margaret did not survive. My mother was not the eldest daughter—she was the middle child—living in the shadow of unmourned loss.

My Mom grew up feeling out of sync with classmates who had younger mothers. She'd told me many times about thick, brown woolen stockings she'd been given to wear that seemed to symbolize her mother's own disconnect from the times. Mom also felt her younger sister, Florence, was the golden child—the artist whose talents were recognized and encouraged. This was not her imagination. Late in life, my grandmother told my mother that she'd never really bonded with her. She'd believed that my mother—like the baby Margaret—would leave her too.

My mother was a bright and beautiful young woman. Her father had encouraged her to leave their small town in Pennsylvania and go away to college. At Syracuse University, my mother would gain more freedom and escape the confines of a distant but over-protective mother. There she met an expanded world—and my father.

Although my mother now lay in a hospital bed, not fully conscious, I believed that she could still hear and feel me. "Today is Father's Day," I said. "Ruth, Carolyn, and I have all talked with Dad."

I'd lived most of my adult life away from my parents, and most of my childhood memories included my father. Wherever my mother was now, I wanted to fill her with lovely memories. I spoke of the house they'd built together in Belle Isle ... the giant blossoms of the magnolia tree in our back yard ... my love of following the paths in the surrounding woods.

As thoughts of my mother's life receded, I readied to leave the hospital. Standing next to her bed, I repeated what had become a ritual with variations. "I am here, and Ruth and Carolyn are at your house, but they are here in your circle of love. Dad and Judy are holding you in their thoughts. Paul and Howard [my sisters' husbands] are too. Whether they are here or there, we are all in your circle of love." She nodded and pursed her lips, as if to kiss the air.

Sisters. Carolyn made a beautiful dinner that evening that the three of us shared. I was surprised to learn that when

Ruth visited that afternoon, Mom was awake and verbal. "She seemed like she wanted to share a secret," Ruth said.

Between the usual interruptions, Mom talked about a party "... where all the people who love each other are together." She wanted us all to go and have fun. "Paul, Carolyn, Howard, and your father are all at the party," Mom confided. "Is Judy there too?" Not knowing about my words with Mom earlier, Ruth corrected her about who was actually in Santa Barbara. Mom replied, "I'm ready to go to the party ... I don't think people do this very often ..."

I think she was right. We had come together in a very special way—each of us having our own shared and private moments with Mom. Of her three daughters, Ruth is the most reserved and had a more distant relationship with our mother. That afternoon, Ruth crawled onto the hospital bed and lay down beside her.

Carolyn and I returned to the hospital that night. I stayed only a moment. Carolyn had not had any time alone with Mom that day. As I readied to leave, Mom was curled on her side. I placed her furry friend, the scraggly lion, next to her and kissed her on the temple.

Each time I saw my mother, I never knew if it would be the last.

Monday, June 19. 3:00 AM. I awoke suddenly in the middle of the night and wondered, "Is it *time*?" Carolyn's name was on the whiteboard in the hospital room. If our mother was in distress, Carolyn would receive the call. I considered calling the nurses' station, but if I did, it might result in unwanted interventions. I also knew from the Shared Crossing Project that some people are unable to pass when loved ones are present. If this *was* my mother's time, our shared crossing would be in the realm of the heart. As if to beckon them, I lay in bed thinking of the people most important in my mother's life as I drifted back to sleep.

I was jarred awake around 3:30 AM to a bright light in the living room and the clear thought, "This is it!" The lamp on the end table next to the couch was flickering. That lamp had poor wiring or a faulty switch, had I remembered to turn it off? —Or was this my mother passing through? I lay frozen in bed, unsure of what to do. I thought, "If the party Mom has been talking about is going on—hers is coming to an end."

When I was able, I stumbled into the living room and unplugged the lamp. As I lay back in bed, I was surprised to feel a softness on the left side of my body and, next to my head, a sense of warmth and love. As I stayed with the feeling, it felt like my mother's love for me, not my love for her—as if she was cradling my cheek. I was wide awake— my experience was not coming from a dreamlike state. One way or another, this was part of our shared crossing.

Carolyn, too, had awoken in the middle of the night, but there was no call from the hospital. Mom was still with us, and our journey continued.

"Dr. B" Revisited.

Early Monday morning, Ruth, Carolyn, and I were back at the hospital to intercept Dr. B on his rounds. We needed to confer on what the progression from the hospital to skilled nursing, palliative care, or hospice might look like. Our experiences with Mom over the weekend had dissolved any of my defensiveness towards Dr. B. There was something much larger and more important going on.

When Dr. B arrived, he pulled us into the hallway to discuss our mother's condition. "It's still too early to tell if she will recover," he said. "It could go either way … it's difficult to predict, but it doesn't look good." He went on to explain that they had done everything they could in the hospital, and medications were not working. Mom needed to be moved into skilled nursing. There she would be given oxygen, but they would not force-feed her. If she did not perk up and was unable to feed herself, he expected that she would pass within a few days. Low doses of morphine would be provided for her comfort.

In other words—Mom was going directly into palliative care.

As Dr. B spoke, my sisters and I stood side-by-side, our arms around each other. We talked about quality of life to let him know that we were in agreement and in it together. Dr. B remarked, "She may have already declared herself." On television and in real life, doctors declare a time of death. I understood him to mean that she might be choosing to die. I stumbled over my words as I tried to say that I knew I had frustrated him the week before … but Dr. B was calm and kind. He touched my back gently as we turned to go into my mother's room. The man who had felled the tree in his office was trying to set it right.

On the Move ...

Our mother was transferred from Cottage Hospital to Valle Verde Health Center that same day. Valle Verde is a retirement community that provides full spectrum care—from independent living to tending the dying. Valle Verde was ideal. It is surrounded by lush gardens and the comfort of familiarity. Directly next to the Health Center was the theater where my mother and I attended talks during symphony season—a tradition we'd shared for many years.

"It's still too early to tell ... it could go either way ..." The words of Dr. B echoed in my mind. With an uncertain future, my sisters and I hoped for the best and prepared for the worst. It is not an easy task to take apart a life, not knowing when or if you will put it back together again. I canceled the planned move to Wood Glen Hall, hoping Mom would recover and a space would still be available. We proceeded as if a move *would* happen—separating out what to put into storage from what to discard, donate, or put in the estate sale. The work was both practical and emotional. Fragments of a life that existed before we were born and long after we left home passed through our hands. We each chose what we wanted to keep that held memories of Mom and the home we grew up in.

The Resurrection ...

Remarkably, with no further medical treatment at Valle Verde—Mom began to recover. Before returning to New York, Carolyn made a beautiful memory book for Mom, filled with photos and captions that told the story of her life. Mom received it with great pleasure and took pride in showing it to all her caregivers. I hoped that it would support her memory and help the staff to understand the person, not just the patient they were caring for.

I am fortunate that my work as a psychotherapist allowed me to control my own schedule. While Mom began physical and occupational therapy, Ruth and I visited consignment stores and met with moving and estate clearance companies. Signs of Mom's recovery were looking good. Physical and occupational therapy at first was rudimentary: getting out of bed, being able to put on her own shoes, and then walking with assistance. Mom was not supposed to do any of these things without supervision to prevent falls and injury. If her call light went unanswered, however, Mom got out of bed and tottered up to the nurses' desk to inform them that she needed to go to the bathroom. I don't know if it was rebellion or if she was doing her best to play by the rules.

Soon, my mother was allowed to move about the Health Center and began attending activities. At a concert of Native American flute music, she was able to play alongside the performer. In Texas, she had been a member of a Native American flute group and had quite a flute collection of her own.

With Mom making good progress, Ruth and I met with the social worker at Valle Verde. We were given a list of assisted living places she thought would be most appropriate for Mom "as a social, outgoing, and popular resident."

Along with the good news came a sobering reality. We

learned that although Medicare covers treatment in skilled nursing for up to a hundred days—that applies only in extreme cases. We did not have much time. Once their team determined Mom's activities of daily living (ADLs) were back to baseline, or she reached a plateau with no improvements over the course of a week—we would receive 48-hour notice to find a new placement. Mom was welcome to stay at Valle Verde—at a cost of more than $11,000 a month, which did not include any further treatment.

Hoping to slow the clock, we provided information on Mom's pre-illness functioning to give a realistic view of her baseline. I stressed the importance of focus on cognitive functioning when determining her readiness for release. I was nervous. I had spoken with Mom's physical therapist, and he thought the speech therapy Mom had just begun could center on that. However, neither the social worker nor the speech therapist was aware of that as a goal. "Specialization" has its limits. In skilled nursing, they work as a team, but each member can do their job and still not hold the big picture—especially when it comes to memory issues.

The work of patient advocacy never really ends.

The team at Valle Verde was optimistic about Mom's capabilities. With a release date imminent, our priority shifted to identifying options in Santa Barbara and New York—in case Mom no longer qualified for Wood Glen Hall. We needed to make decisions based on her resources and long-term care policy—without knowing how long those resources would need to last.

Alone Again.

With Carolyn and Ruth back in New York, I continued to prepare for the estate clearance. On my visits to Valle Verde, I took along items that might have meaning to Mom, hoping for help with decisions about what to toss or to keep. Instead, it proved to be a source of conversation. One day, I brought in her high school graduation album. Unlike yearbooks of today, it held only a few pictures and consisted mostly of business-sized cards engraved with the names of each student and teacher. Mom pointed to one of the cards and said, "That's the gym teacher who was messing with some of the girls." I was astonished. Although Mom's short-term memory was poor, her long-term memory was remarkable.

Ultimately, the owner of the estate company would separate out what he thought they could sell from what his team would drop at a thrift store or take to the dump. It's not easy to part with items you've known for a lifetime. A few from the donation pile made their way back to my apartment. As the truck pulled away, I was left with nearly empty rooms. All that remained was clearing the debris and turning in the keys.

Back at Valle Verde, an appointment was set with the Director and head nurse of Wood Glen Hall. They would come to the Health Center to assess whether Mom was still appropriate for their facility. Wood Glen Hall does not admit people in wheelchairs or with dementia. I was cautiously optimistic. Mom was fully mobile and still had a diagnosis of mild cognitive impairment. She'd managed to slip out of the Health Center to get ice cream at the community dining hall next door and find her way back again. Before the interview, I coached Mom to listen carefully to what they asked. She could be charming and entertaining, but I feared she might talk about herself with little relevance to their questions ... I really needed it to work.

July 7, 2017. On the day of the interview, my mother and I sat waiting on a couch outside of the conference room. Although my mother struggled with memory, she was still capable of coherent and meaningful conversations. She turned towards me and said, "All this will come to an end."

"I know," I said softly. "I think you are at peace with that, and so am I."

During the interview, my mother was accepted to Wood Glen Hall and a move-in date was set for July 11. The next day I oversaw the move of Mom's possessions out of storage and began setting up her room. I was greeted by residents we'd met on our first visit who were now enthusiastically anticipating her arrival. After I helped a future neighbor find her keys and open her door, my confidence began to grow. The woman across the hall had difficulty speaking and had likely suffered a stroke. The director confided that it was not unusual for residents to hide things for safekeeping and then forget where they'd put them. My mother would not be alone in her memory challenges. Outside the dining hall, I counted almost as many walkers as there were rooms. My Mom would be a track star!

TRAGEDY OF ERRORS:
Disaster at
Wood Glen Hall

July 11, 2017. One month after my mother became seriously ill, I drove her to Wood Glen Hall—the place I hoped would become her new and final home. As I unpacked her bags, the nurse arrived to deliver a safety pendant and the number for the front desk so that Mom could call for help at any time. While the nurse was still there, the fire alarm in the room went off, and several staff responded immediately. There was no fire—just a false alarm. This now feels like an omen of things to come.

Mom and I had lunch in the dining hall with her table-mates. Zanita, one of the loveliest women you could ever hope to meet, was also an official member of the Welcoming Committee. It was clear that she was taking Mom under her wing. At lunch, Mom went back and forth between chatting in a friendly manner, then searching for words and having difficulty being understood. When I left for work, Mom was settled in her room, surrounded by the warmth of familiar things.

I had some concern that day about whether Mom would be able to orient herself to a new environment—but at Wood Glen Hall, it was a straight shot down the hall to the dining room and activity centers. Her name and room number were on her safety pendant so that any staff member or fellow resident could serve as a guide. If lost, she would be found. Zanita lived halfway down the hall and would accompany Mom to dinner and back that evening.

I emailed both of my sisters to fill them in on the plan so that they could help support the transition. Ruth called Mom just before dinner to remind her that Zanita was coming to take her to the dining room. Ruth needed to repeat this several times. That evening, Carolyn reported that Mom was in good spirits and seemed comfortable in her room—although she was anxious about whether something had happened to me. Mom wondered when I would return. Carolyn explained that I was working late and would not be coming back that night. She reminded Mom of an exercise she'd learned at Valle Verde, "Breathe in like you are smelling brownies ... breathe out like you are blowing out birthday candles." With that happy image, Mom seemed calm when they said goodnight.

My anxiety about Mom's adjustment to her new surroundings receded behind a wave of exhaustion. I barely knew what day it was. I did not have the luxury of weekdays and weekends—every day was MOM-day. I worked until almost 8 PM, bought a pint of Häagen-Dazs, and returned home in hopes of finding the mind I had lost weeks before—my own. The signs of impending disaster were there, but I could not read them.

When I arrived at Wood Glen Hall the next morning, the director and the nurse headed toward me, visibly alarmed. The physical therapist had arrived to assess my mother and found her in such a distressed state that they were now trying to figure out what had happened. "Maybe you can help."

I knelt down next to my mother, who was huddled in a chair in the hallway. All available staff gathered around us. Mom's words poured out in an incoherent jumble ... something about being locked out of her room ... people wouldn't let her in ... or out ... being in the hall ... no one came.

She was trembling. Terrified.

With me there, Mom began to calm down. Though she was never fully coherent, I was able to piece together a picture of her experience—though not necessarily what actually happened. She said she had used her safety pendant twice and no one came. She felt mistreated by the staff that did come. I thought this was unlikely ... she also talked about me "going off down the road with two girls laughing" and leaving her behind.

"Who were the two girls?" I asked. She didn't know. It seemed our lunch with her tablemates and conversations with my sisters may have melded into one. Dementia means living in a land where time and space take on a life of its own. It was clear she felt afraid and abandoned.

The physical therapist who had arrived that morning explained that there was a diagnosis of encephalopathy in Mom's chart, "Maybe it's gotten worse." Encephalopathy? What chart? No one had ever mentioned that to me—and what did it mean?

From my own experience with the leadership, staff, and residents at Wood Glen Hall, I trusted that everyone was trying to help. With a plan in place, I had to leave for work. I had a fourteen-year-old client with a history of trauma waiting in my office and no way to reach her. Someone would stay with Mom at all times while the director called her doctor to determine whether she should be taken to the emergency room or back to Valle Verde. I promised to return as quickly as possible.

When I arrived back at Wood Glen Hall, everyone—the director, the nurse, and myself—was upset. Dr. B had informed them that my mother had "Alzheimer's transitive dementia." He was surprised they had accepted her. They were perturbed—Wood Glen Hall does not accept residents with dementia. They'd been instructed that Mom should not be taken to the hospital. Valle Verde would re-admit her under private pay—it would not be covered by Medicare.

From what my mother was able to communicate and conversations with staff and other residents over the course of the day—a likely version of what happened that night began to emerge. It seemed that my mother had gotten up in the middle of the night, and the newly-painted bathroom door was stuck due to the heat and humidity of summer. Panicked, she went out the front door of her room, and it closed behind her. Lost in unfamiliar surroundings and unable to get back in, she was convinced that someone was trying to keep her out.

The director had already spoken to the night staff that

responded to Mom's calls and returned her to her room. When the morning crew arrived to take her to breakfast, Mom was sitting in her room in the dark. Still in the grip of fear, she believed that someone was stopping her from turning on the light. At breakfast, she tried to eat oatmeal with a fork … She was a mess.

I learned from a resident that her confusion had been evident the night before. After dinner, she was convinced that I and "two girls" were coming with food, even though she had just eaten. Mom also told me that "a lot of noise and a party was going on that night." I believe that there was a commotion—but it was happening inside a ravaged mind.

There was no "comedy of errors" that night, only the tragedy that unfolded. I had noticed the stickiness of the door earlier but failed to bring it to anyone's attention. Wood Glen Hall had come to Valle Verde to assess my mother but did not ask for a new physician's statement before accepting her. I was the primary holder of power of attorney and responsible for making medical decisions. If there were any changes to her diagnosis, no one had communicated that to me. We will never really know everything that happened that night, but the dream of my mother living out her years in that lovely community—in one night—became a nightmare.

That dawn brought a glaringly harsh reality. My mother, who had lived independently only a month before, was now not reliably capable of taking care of herself, unprompted or unsupervised. She was not appropriate to Wood Glen Hall, and they would not accept her back.

THE SEARCH FOR "HOME"

July 12, 2017. I drove my mother back to Valle Verde under a facade of calm in hopes she might feel safe and cared for. Once Mom was settled in her room, I met with the social worker to sort out what had happened and why. I understood the purpose of skilled nursing was to bring patients back to baseline or stabilized. I was confused about the conditions of my mother's release. Mom was clearly not back to baseline, and I hoped her condition could still improve.

A review of my mother's file showed no notes about encephalopathy, dementia, or Alzheimer's. Valle Verde was treating bronchiectasis, pneumonia, and failure to thrive. Team meetings were focused on those illnesses and her activities of daily living (ADLs). Her ability to get up, get dressed, feed herself, and walk was the basis of her discharge. Little, if any, attention had been given to her cognitive functioning. During that meeting, I learned a hard truth. Medicare covers skilled nursing for acute illness—it does not cover issues related to dementia.

I was advised I could advocate for a "failed discharge," and the team would make a decision within the next few days. If successful, that might buy us a little time, but my sisters and I jumped into action. We needed to review Mom's long-term care policy in order to develop a plan. Mom's policy had an "exclusion period" of 180 days, which meant none of her care would be covered during that time. We needed to get the clock ticking as quickly as possible. Ruth and Carolyn took on that task while I packed up Mom's belongings at Wood Glen Hall and moved them back into storage.

In the twists and turns of fate, I learned that the two best options I had identified in Santa Barbara had no openings. We needed to consider other options in both Santa Barbara and New York. I researched and visited several facilities—none of which looked like good, long-term solutions. Ruth and Carolyn re-visited places we had considered out east and put a deposit down on one.

July 15, 2017. Mom was settling into familiar surroundings at Valle Verde. She was sad and deflated, but she was not afraid—she knew where she was. "Ramon gives the symphony talks here," she said. She looked forward to seeing him again in August. "He will pay attention to me."

Mom had conversations with Carolyn that she did not have with me. Mom was still haunted by what had happened at Wood Glen Hall. She talked about "that night"—a noise she couldn't get away from ... waking up in a snowstorm ... people being against her ...

Mom was confused about how she had gotten to Valle Verde. "The world is here, but I can't work in it … I feel bad for people with minds and no place to go." Mom said she wasn't holding it against us, "I'm not putting anything on you … don't have anything bad for you … I'm not suffering." Then she told Carolyn, "I want to get out of here tomorrow."

Carolyn could only reply, "That's not going to happen."

All I could do was reassure Mom that we were working hard to find the best possible place for her to live—close to Ruth and Carolyn in New York or close to me in Santa Barbara.

July 18, 2017. I stared into the cap of a bottle of Organic Honest Tea, reading a quote by William Shakespeare: "There is nothing either good or bad, only thinking makes it so."

I picked up the phone and called a former professor who was now the Director at the Center for Successful Aging in Santa Barbara. I hoped he would have suggestions for temporary placements while we weighed our options. After I described our predicament, he said he did not think that Mom needed to be in memory care. "Most residents in assisted living struggle with memory loss but do not require a locked unit." As it turned out, he was one of the owners of Alexander Gardens, one of the assisted living facilities I was interested in. "Most of our residents learn the layout within a few days." The Director at Alexander Gardens had run a large memory care unit in Los Angeles and won awards for sensory integration programs for patients with dementia. "I'll give him a call," he said. Although Alexander Gardens currently had no openings, the wait time was generally between 12 and 15 weeks. I was new to this. I was so focused on long-term care that the rapid turnover in assisted living had never occurred to me.

Later that day, Ruth called with good news. Mom's claim for long-term care had been approved. Her hospitalization and time in skilled nursing would count towards her exclusion period. I could breathe again. In five months, most of her expenses would be covered and we would no longer be hemorrhaging money. We now had time to find the best, most appropriate living situation without fear of exhausting all her resources.

The next day I met with the social worker at Valle Verde and learned Medicare coverage would expire at midnight on July 20. I let her know of our decision to keep Mom at Valle Verde until we could determine the next best step. We also needed a new, more accurate physician's report. My mother was not the only one still haunted by the night at Wood Glen Hall. I did not want to risk another move that might add to her distress and confusion.

July 26, 2017. I received news of two openings at Alexander Gardens. One room was available for respite care, and another was being refurbished and would become available shortly. I visited the same day. Could this be a dream come true? Alexander Gardens seemed just that—a charming old mansion surrounded by gardens and clusters of cottages that rose up a gentle hill.

"The Gardens" looked like the best choice in Santa Barbara, but the question remained ... what was the best option? Santa Barbara or New York? What would be best for Mom, and for me?

I felt the quality of personal care would be better in a smaller place like Alexander Gardens. However, the larger, more corporate option in New York would be balanced by the presence of family and a memory care unit if that was needed in the future. I emailed my sisters to schedule a conference call. This was a decision we would need to make together.

When I went into the conference call, I was leaning toward New York. I was exhausted, and I'd come to terms with a possible move east before my mother became ill. Still, I could not in good conscience move Mom to New York without asking, "Is having Mom there something you really want ... are you willing to take it on?" I knew what an undertaking it would be.

I was determined to be at peace with whatever decision was made.

My question became irrelevant when Carolyn arrived on the call with news that the center in New York would only accept Mom into memory care. A decision was made. I called Alexander Gardens and scheduled an assessment. If Mom was not accepted there, we would move her into memory care in New York.

July 31, 2017. The assessment at Alexander Gardens consisted of lunch with residents and conversations with the

Director, Co-Director, Care Coordinator, nurse, and various staff. Mom liked the available room, and the staff liked her. Mom was accepted, and a move-in date was set. On August 2, I left her belongings in storage and moved her into respite care. After the disaster at Wood Glen Hall, I was not sure if this placement would stick.

"THE GARDENS"

August 2, 2017. I moved my mother into Alexander Gardens, still vigilant for everything that could go wrong. Fearing a repeat of Wood Glen Hall, I asked, "Should I stay with her for the first couple of nights?" They assured me that would not be necessary. There was a secure perimeter, and the night staff would check on her every half hour.

In many ways, Mom's adjustment went smoothly. She liked her room and learned the lay of the land quickly. Ritual and routine were the mainstays at Alexander Gardens—a whiteboard in the dining room posted the activities of the day. Staff came to Mom's room and invited her to participate in programs or escort her to meals. She sat at the same table with the same four women, breakfast, lunch, and dinner. A gentleman at the next table sparked her interest, and she greeted him every time he entered the room. The dining room staff affectionately called Martha "Martita."

A stone wall edged the property, but it was still possible to wander off during the day, for anyone clever or strong enough to lift the heavy iron latch on the front gate. I knew there were two things that could end a stay in assisted living—becoming a wanderer, getting lost and putting yourself in danger, or becoming violent. "Mom, stay close to the house. Don't leave the grounds alone," I cautioned. She received my instructions like a compliant child. I felt that she was in a safe and loving environment.

Within two weeks, I was confident that Mom did not need to be in a locked memory care unit. I was able to schedule the move of her belongings into her room and contract for long-term care. At the end of the month, Mom would become a resident. During my visits, we often sat just outside the dining room under an archway next to a butterfly enclosure. We watched as chrysalises transformed and stretched their nascent wings. I hoped Mom would soon connect with her tablemates and that "The Gardens" would begin to feel like home.

I put laundry tags in her clothes, had cable and phone installed, and got the paperwork for her long-term care in place. With the day-to-day care of Mom shifted onto others, I began to look forward to a life that had been set aside long ago. Oh, how I longed to dance once again. I still called my mother every evening, but daily visits became chats, and shared meals with her happened several times a week.

When I visited for lunch, I sat between my mother and Bea. Bea was a pretty, petite woman with a well-coiffed silver bob. Her son took her to the hairdresser every week ...

though she sometimes called him her husband. On my first visit to Alexander Gardens, I'd learned a little bit about Bea. Her story provided hope for my mother's recovery. Before arriving at Alexander Gardens, Bea had lived alone for some time ... her memory was poor, and she barely spoke. Now I enjoyed sitting next to Bea as she chatted about the book she was reading and the author she liked, saying, "He's so handsome!"

When I was sixteen, I had a summer job in the mountains outside of Aspen, Colorado. On my time off, I'd set sight on a peak and head up the slope. The closer I got to the summit, the more it seemed to recede into the distance ... Finding Mom safe and happy felt that way. When Carolyn made her first visit to Alexander Gardens in September, Mom told her, "I want to get out of here."

Mom was settled ... but she was not happy.

As Mom became more comfortable, she had more complaints. She didn't like all the music programs ... the art projects weren't creative enough ... the woman who lived next door wailed to get the staff's attention. Mom hated Bingo, as she told me every day. The truth was, she couldn't keep up and was miffed when someone reached over to help. Mom grumbled, but I knew what another move would mean—less freedom and less personalized care.

I sat next to my mother, listening to the same complaints I'd heard day after day, when she said, "I don't know if I can keep living here."

I responded simply, "There are no better options ... It

would be great if things could go back to the way they used to be ... but you are not able to live alone and take care of yourself anymore."

Her shoulders slumped, and her eyes grazed the floor in resignation. "I know," she replied.

Mom had her discontents, and I had my own frustrations. The long-term care claims were not being submitted correctly, delaying the payments, despite the template I'd provided from the insurance company. Mom could call me ... then forget to hang up the phone, resulting in concerned emails from my sisters. Mom had difficulty turning on her television and changing channels, so practice became part of our routine during our evening calls.

To remedy the situation, I created simple, color-coded instructions, with large print and pictures that I posted on her wall—then glued big colored dots onto her remote control and telephone receiver. I'd done this successfully back in March when Mom got hearing aids. Handouts—and practice, practice, practice—it had worked then. I was determined to teach Mom to do things for herself that could make her life better. Help and repeat—that was my strategy—this time to no avail. Mom forgot to look at the handouts or could not move from one simple step to the next. Her capacities were declining, although it was difficult to see clearly at the time. In some moments, she seemed so capable and, in the next, utterly helpless. Dementia is a confusing and devious beast.

Mom's complaints were mixed with distress. I became concerned when she said, "I don't think people are being well cared for ..."

"What do you mean?" I asked.

"After dinner, they are left in their wheelchairs in the living room ... and there's no staff." I thought it likely that staff were nearby, clearing the dining room or in the kitchen. Still, I did not want to dismiss her concerns when she told me that she pressed the call buttons on others' safety pendants to summon help. Whether or not they needed help—I did not know.

It was difficult to separate quality of care issues from Mom's problems in understanding what was actually happening around her. At Ruth's urging, I made an appointment to meet with the Co-Director and Care Coordinator. Ruth works in the medical field, and she reminded me, "People with families involved get better care ... The squeaky wheel gets the grease."

On the evening before the meeting, I was able to instruct Mom to pick up the white remote control with large buttons I'd special-ordered and get her to the right channel for her evening show. Success! However, after many tries, I could not get her to put down the remote control and hang up the phone. Instead, she kept holding the remote to her ear and inadvertently changing channels or turning off the TV. After helping her several times to turn on the TV and get back to her show—I still could not get her to hang up the phone. In exasperation, I snapped. "Stop talking! ... Listen! ... Put the white thing down on the table next to you! Take the black thing away from your ear and push the red button ... I can't do this!" Somehow, miraculously—she hung up on me.

I felt terrible. "Patience ... let go of expectations ...

meet them where they are ..." I'm a therapist. I know these things ... but that night? I'd lost it. I felt like the mother who yells at her child because they don't yet know how to tie their own shoes.

In the last few months, I'd put Mom in the hospital, cleared Mom's apartment, moved her in and out of Wood Glen Hall, back to Valle Verde, into Alexander Gardens for respite, and then arranged long-term care. I sat with clients' problems during the day. How was I to manage my own stress, work, and take care of Mom?

Meeting at Alexander Gardens ...

The next morning, I sat across the desk from Mary, the Co-Director, with Alba, the Care Coordinator at my side. The paperwork issues that required a meeting to resolve had not instilled confidence. I was exhausted and emotionally drained. For my own peace of mind, I knew I needed to understand what was happening at Alexander Gardens. What was the quality of care my mother was receiving? What was Mom actually capable of doing on her own? I made a silent vow to listen closely to the people who were with her every day. Their observations could be a gift.

The tension in my body began to dissolve as Mary and Alba answered my questions. The following is a composite of what I learned that day.

"Your mother is experienced as pleasant by the staff ... She spends most of the day in the main house and greets all the residents as they come and go ... She likes most of the music programs ... When she is not participating in activities, she watches, listens, and makes good comments ... She's good about using her pendant to call staff and communicating if she's dizzy or not feeling well. She needs to be prompted to get to meals ... The staff reminds her to make her bed ... She receives assistance bathing ..."

"She doesn't sun-down, but she's different in the morning than later in the day when she's less coherent." Sundowning is common for people with Alzheimer's. As the light fades at the end of the day, restlessness, agitation, distress, and confusion may begin or intensify. This can cause difficulty sleeping, which exacerbates the problem and their misery. Thankfully, this was not happening for Mom.

I laughed when Alba said, "She wants to wear the same green sweater every day. The caregivers try to help her pick out something else so they can wash it." That green chenille sweater was so loved by Mom that the fuzz had worn off its shoulders.

Mary asked, "Would you like the laundry to lose it?" I'd had the same thought many times, but familiarity was comfort for Mom. That sweater would continue its life in the wardrobe.

It became clear that Alba was not a supervisor who stayed behind a desk. She knew my mother well. "She's a helper. *She wants to be in control* ... Your mother reminds us of what she used to do, working with people and children ... Sometimes she pushes the button on other people's pendants if she thinks they need help."

Mary shared that it is common for family members to receive all the complaints. "Time is a gray area for most of the residents, and they will perseverate. You will hear the same things over and over again." As she spoke, I thought of children who hold it together for the teacher, then want to go wild when they get home. I had become the receptacle for all my mother's frustrations that came with the ongoing loss of her capacities.

I was shocked when Mary said, "Your mother is considered to be high functioning with mild cognitive impairment."

"Really?" I exclaimed.

When I described my hair-pulling moment on the phone the night before, Mary said, "Your mother can only think about one thing at a time. Three commands are too many." Perhaps to reassure me, she went on to say, "This is difficult to do in your own family ... Alba is unflappable and endlessly patient with the residents ..."

Alba piped up, "And then when I get home, I want to yell at my kid, 'Go sit in your chair!'"

"Think about your mother as a new person," Mary said. "This is not the same person you used to know."

By the end of the meeting, I was tired but relieved. I felt confident in their expertise and the quality of care my mother was receiving.

Outside the window, I caught sight of my mother sitting in the courtyard waiting to go in to lunch. Despite the bright sunlight and butterflies that flitted nearby, a heaviness surrounded her. Mom's head and shoulders drooped as I sat down next to her. She may have forgotten the things I'd said, but it was clear she remembered how it felt. My heart broke as she talked of how badly she felt about herself and what she could not do. If anyone was to carry the shame of that night, I felt it should be me. All I could do was to say, "I'm sorry." There was a tenderness between us as I assured her that I'd spoken to the staff. "Things are okay ... and they can get better." To lighten the mood, I reminded her, "We have something to look forward to ... I'll pick you up on Friday, and we'll go see Ramon at the Symphony Talk."

Trial by Fire ...

December 4, 2017. I was beginning to let go and let the staff do their jobs when fast-moving wildfires ignited southern California. The Thomas Fire reached the city of Ventura less than thirty miles away, destroying over five hundred homes in a single night. In the days that followed, fires burned through the Santa Ynez Mountains and crept up the coast toward Santa Barbara. Alexander Gardens formulated an evacuation plan, and I packed a bag for Mom to be ready to go.

December 16, 2017. Alexander Gardens was now only one block away from an evacuation zone. With high winds fanning the flames, it felt like anything could happen. Instead of waiting for a call in the middle of the night, I decided to move Mom up the coast—for her health and to escape the suspense that seemed to thread through every hour.

The acrid smell of smoke hung in the air as we joined the caravan inching its way along clogged routes out of town. Police cars stood sentinel at the entrance to neighborhoods already evacuated—to prevent looting and the foolishness of those wanting to get closer for a better look. I gripped the wheel and tried to maintain a calm, upbeat manner as my mother repeatedly asked where we were going and why. I answered with variations, "There is a fire, but we are safe … We're taking a little trip to keep you healthy … We're going to a lovely town on the beach." Her memory could not hold.

"What gave you the idea to go?" she asked.

I was on my last nerve when Mom said, "I'd do much better if I lived on my own." Mom could not reliably use her phone, needed prompting to go to meals, and needed assistance bathing.

"No, Mom, you are not capable of living on your own."

Irritation mixed with melancholy as she spoke. "I don't think you respect what I can do."

"I respect what you've done and what you can do … but I also see what you can't do for yourself …" Then, with a definitive tone, "We're not going to discuss it."

"When will we get there?" she asked.

"We'll be there soon," I replied, time and time again.

When we arrived at the hotel in Pismo Beach, I unpacked the back of my car stuffed with belongings in case my apartment burned to the ground in our absence. Over the next few days, activities distracted from a land on fire—and the challenge of holding a conversation. We ate our first breakfast at Old West Cinnamon Rolls, had lunch and dinner near the beach, and did a little Christmas shopping amidst sunshine and palm trees. In a store that specialized in fun socks, I brought Mom's attention to a sale on her favorite brand of orthopedic shoes. She fingered the shoes tentatively as she said, "... I might not have any feet..." What struck me as strange then—now seems prophetic.

One evening, I risked a short walk alone to the pier. The deep orange of sunset was tinged with worry that Mom might wander out of the hotel room and become lost in town. When I returned, she greeted me with a smile, and we picked through a bounty of leftovers from our eating expeditions.

Mom needed to be prompted to cut up her food, flush the toilet, and wash her hands. When she took naps or went to bed early, I tracked the fires on the news and binge-watched Netflix. Amidst the tensions, there were lovely moments, too. We spent time on the boardwalk watching children play in the sand ... found the Butterfly Park and peered through a telescope at monarchs high in the eucalyptus trees. I was surprised when Mom remembered being in the grove years before, when we'd visited her Aunt Gail in a nearby town.

December 19, 2017. By Monday morning, it felt safe enough to return to Santa Barbara. As I drove, I sought solace in the landscape of rolling hills dotted with oak trees. Mom couldn't understand where we were going or what would be there when we arrived. Still, she was concerned that she would be in trouble for leaving. I assured her that they knew where she was and that she was with me. "You'll still have your room, with all your things when we get there ... You'll be there in time for lunch."

"Will you drive back tonight?" she asked.

"No, Mom. I live in Santa Barbara, just five minutes from you."

As I drove up the street to my office, a swath of blackened earth marked the hillside above, left barren by the fire that weekend.

"Transfer Trauma"

December 20, 2017. My phone rang early the next morning, and Mom was on the line. Although she could not reliably tell the difference between her telephone and the remote control—she always remembered how to call me. With a mind still clouded with sleep, it was words, not eggs, that were scrambled that morning. Mom sounded troubled as she tried to tell me about a trip she had taken "with a man ... We had our own cars ... there were two beds ..." True to her Victorian background, she made a point of telling me there was no sex involved: "He didn't touch me ..."

Other details held fragments of people and places that could have landed her anywhere in space or time. My heart ripped through whatever exhaustion remained from the weekend as I said gently, "Mom, you did go on a trip ... that trip was with me ... You don't have a car anymore. I drove ... *We* had two beds ..." Now fully awake, I said, "I think your mind is mixing dreams and memories with the trip we took this weekend ..." I had a client scheduled that morning but promised to be there as soon as I could.

As I sat next to Mom on her single bed, she tried to unravel a tangle of memories: "The place 'he' went to school ... a wedding ... a party ... a young man ... We went on a trip ...” she said. “We each had our own car ... I drove myself.”

I asked, “Are you talking about a memory?”

No, these were things she thought she had done that day. Certainty and confusion had taken up residence side by side in her mind.

Clearly, Mom was in orbit, and I wanted to bring her back to earth. I tried to separate the past and present by reminding her of the trip we had taken and all the things we’d done together. Wherever she was in her mind, I wanted her to know that she was not alone. “I am here, and I live only a few minutes away.”

For Mom, a deeper fear surfaced. She asked, “How many of you are here?”

“Just me,” I said. “Carolyn and Ruth are in New York.”

With eyes downcast, she replied, “They should stay there ...”

“Why should they stay?” I asked.

“They shouldn’t have to deal with me ...” Her tone hung with gloom as she went on to say, “I don’t want any friends to visit ... I don’t want them to see me this way ... I don’t make sense ...”

“Ruth and Carolyn are planning to come soon for your birthday ... I’m sure they want to see you.”

I hoped a return to routine and the familiar would restore Mom’s confidence. I tried to shift her attention to what she did know and understand. “You remembered that the therapy dog came today. That was real ... You know Bea and Jean. They will sit next to you when you go down to lunch."

Before I left Alexander Gardens, I described what was happening to one of the staff. She did not seem particularly concerned, "We see things like this all the time." Later, I would learn from the nurse about "*transfer trauma*." What I saw is common among people with dementia and can be brought on by something as simple as a trip to the doctor. We had been gone for days.

After I sent a lengthy email to my sisters, Ruth called Mom to see how she was doing. "Not good," she told Ruth. "I had nerve skunk around noon." (No, this is not a typo; this is what she said.) Mom was still talking about going on a trip: "to the country … where he went to school." Then Mom said, "I'm stuck … not thinking right … Deb talked me through it …" Mom again feared being a burden to others, saying, "I can't entertain anything going on, and I'm really sad about it."

The next day I went back to Alexander Gardens to check in with Alba. Mom had been checked for fever and UTI, either of which could contribute to confusion. Mom had neither—but was asking for her father and wondering why he wasn't there.

I found Mom sitting in the living room next to Bea, listening to the music program of the day. There was a glimmer of a return to normalcy as I took a place on the floor at her feet. Roderick, the Native American man she'd played flute with at Valle Verde, now sat at a keyboard singing Christmas songs punctuated with the occasional trumpet solo.

When I spoke with Mom afterward, her speech was

more coherent, and she seemed content. She was still talking about a trip with a young man, but she was not distressed—even after I said, "That must be a memory. The only trip you've taken recently was with me."

"I wish I could get the pictures out of my head," she replied.

As I walked Mom into the dining room, she said, "I know I need to be here ... I can accept it." But then again, she thought she was leaving with me.

She was surprised when I said, "No, Mom, you live here ... You'll have lunch here and will again tomorrow."

As Mom settled into her place at the table, Bea leaned into me and whispered, "Your daughter is feeling better today."

THE BEGINNING
OF THE END

Friday, December 29, 2017.

It was the Friday before New Year's Eve. After work, I went to visit my mother, hoping to spend a little time with her before going to a holiday party that evening. When I entered her room, I found her sitting in her rocking chair, appearing half asleep. "Hi, Mom." A pleasant look of recognition crossed her face, but words did not come easily.

I flopped down on her single bed atop a family quilt, fingering the tiny stitches made by the hands of a lost generation. Mom could be slow in moving between sleep and fully awakened states, so I tried to engage her in conversation. I needed her to be fully alert before our walk down the gentle slope to the dining room. An ominous feeling crept in as she faded in and out. She was not becoming more clear or coherent. She was not waking up.

Déjà vu. Memories of June came flooding back, and her history of pneumonia propelled me into action. I knew her doctor's office would have closed early for the holidays. Past experience had taught me that immediate action was necessary to prevent a downward spiral. If not taken, whatever recovery was possible would be compromised.

I rushed down to the office to call her doctor's after-hours line. I sat glued to a chair, awaiting a call from Dr. B—fearing a repeat of his wrath in June. In what felt like a new "state of emergency," memories of his finer moments did not come to mind. One does not think clearly in moments like these. I could have called from my mother's room, but I also wanted the staff to know what was happening. I felt torn between being with my mother and completing the task at hand. Fortunately, Dr. B returned my call quickly with assurances that a prescription would go to the pharmacy for what we assumed was a repeat of her respiratory problems.

I took deep breaths as I drove, trying to calm myself. When I arrived at the pharmacy, they could find no record of the prescription. I explained the seriousness of the situation and that it could not wait until Monday. "Please call her doctor." I fumbled through my purse and handed them a slip of paper. "I have his number right here ... I spoke to him only half an hour ago." The pharmacy tech looked at me and informed me that *they do not do such things.* Armed with a large dose of desperation and determination, I plopped myself down into the blood pressure chair. "I'm not leaving until the problem is solved."

After what felt like an eternity, my name was called. The order had been processed and was ready to go. I don't know whether a fax came in or a call was made. It didn't really matter. Back in Mom's room, I handed the medication over to her sweet caregiver, David, feeling that somehow disaster had been averted.

I arrived the next morning, hoping for signs that the antibiotics for her chronic respiratory problems had begun to take effect. Instead, I learned that my mother had not been given her medication that day because they did not have the proper paperwork. My mind reeled with the absurdity—I had braved calling the after-hours line on a holiday weekend, taken a stand at the pharmacy, and now bureaucracy was blocking what needed to be done?

There was fear in David's eyes as he rushed towards me to explain. It seemed he was in trouble for "not doing it by the books," having given my mother her medication the night before. We were both so distraught that we could barely hear each other, but somehow came to an understanding. I held power of attorney and would take responsibility for the medical decisions. It was I who was following doctor's orders. I vowed to defend him if it came to that.

I then sat in the office with the charge nurse, trying to sort out the protocol to ensure that my mother received her medications that day. I went home uncertain of the outcome. My mother needed rest, and I needed relief from what felt like temporary insanity (theirs, not mine). Later, when I returned, my mother had been given her medication. We were back on track ... or so I thought.

When I jumped into action on Friday, I assumed that my mother's illness was a repeat of June—another bout of pneumonia that needed to be treated in the same way as in the past. Earlier in the week, a team of paramedics assessing a resident in their room did not strike me as unusual in a place like Alexander Gardens. However, between Friday and Sunday, it seemed like an ambulance was in the driveway every time I came and went. A flu epidemic was hitting Santa Barbara and hitting it hard.

New Year's Eve ...

Sunday, December 31, 2017. When I arrived at my mother's cottage that evening, I could hear a nurse assessing her neighbor next door. I entered my mother's room to find her hunched over a tray that teetered on top of the radiator. I scanned the room for a better place to eat. There was none. David was there, encouraging Mom with a spoonful of mashed potatoes. She was so weak she could barely manage a bite. This felt all too familiar. My heart sank as I realized that the antibiotics were not working.

David left to manage the drama unfolding next door. I helped my mother into her rocking chair and put on a DVD to distract from the commotion outside. A screech and a resounding clunk signaled the arrival of paramedics and the stretcher that would carry her neighbor to the hospital. When the noise subsided, I was left with an agonizing decision.

Should I have my mother taken to the hospital?

Was her weakness a natural part of the dying process that should be allowed to take its course—or an illness from which she could recover? If this was the flu, could she recover and to what extent? Her illness in June had taken a serious toll on her mind—the cost had been a night of terror at Wood Glen Hall. A trip to the hospital might mean her survival, but a return to what quality of life? Thoughts continued to swirl through my mind. I knew that most people prefer to die at home. She certainly would. But without a hospital bed in her room, would she be safe? Whatever I chose, what would it mean? For her—and about me?

When David returned, I tried to consult with him about what to do. David is a gentle soul and looked as distressed as I was. Similar scenes were playing out in more than one room that night. We probably both hoped that someone else would make the decisions—David called Dr. B. I remember none of the details of that conversation but the upshot of it was—I was responsible. It was up to me.

I sat in agony next to my mother as *The Sound of Music* flickered on the screen before us. She looked so fragile and only half aware. Her head bobbed up and down, a faint smile on her face as she tried to mouth the words. Mom seemed to take pleasure in the music ... perhaps memories from the past or the simple fact that I was there. These moments will live forever inside of me with such sweetness and pain.

The anguish of indecision felt like being ripped apart from the inside. The next time David came in, I asked him to call 911. Once the decision was made, I steeled myself for what I knew would come. I was only halfway through the book *It's Okay To Die* by Dr. Monica Williams-Murphy, but I knew what intubation and resuscitation meant—the risks of infection my mother's body was too weak to bear, the low likelihood of survival with resuscitation, and the potential complications such as broken bones and further brain damage. It is with this knowledge that I found my strength and my actions emboldened. At every step of the way, I told the firemen who arrived first, then the paramedics, and later, the nurses and doctors at the hospital, "My mother has a DNR." I approved treatment for her illness, but no extreme measures.

My mother got cold easily, so I grabbed a small quilt and followed the ambulance to the emergency department. When I arrived, my mother was in a room with another patient, separated only by the arc of a curtain—from the murmurings of misery and her cough, likely another victim of the flu. We awaited a battery of blood tests, EKG, and chest X-rays before being moved to a tiny room with one plastic chair wedged between the hospital bed and the wall. A wave of relief came with the arrival of Dr. Andersen, his relaxed smile and jovial manner. He knew my mother! He treated her bouts of pneumonia in 2015 at the urgent care clinic next to her apartment complex. After Dr. Andersen called and consulted with Dr. B, I knew she was in good hands.

My mother would spend that night in the emergency department. There were no beds to be found in a hospital overflowing with flu patients. As I left the hospital that New Year's Eve, a smooth expanse of white marble reached towards the sky and orbs of soft lamplight offered solidity and calm.

2018: THE FINAL JOURNEY

Monday, January 1, 2018.

By the afternoon of New Year's Day, my mother had been moved to a spacious private room in the new part of the hospital. Dispensers with medical masks and hand sanitizer were posted outside every door. The nurse reported that my mother had no fever, and there was nothing significant in her labs beyond the diagnosis of flu type A and pneumonia. I felt I'd made the right decision. Unlike the night before, Mom seemed coherent enough—she was complaining. She didn't think the hospital was being run very well and wanted to know who was in charge—for her, a sure sign of improvement.

The next evening Dr. B called me at home. He said it was too early to know how things would go, but my mother's lungs were a bit clearer. She was too weak to be released back to Alexander Gardens, so he was looking for a bed in skilled nursing. Many facilities were reluctant to admit flu patients, but the hospital would not discharge her without a place to go. I thanked him for being so responsive and on top of things ... Towards the end of our conversation, he said, "She may not make it through this ..."

"... I know," I replied quietly.

I was at peace with that ... and with him.

It is a strange land to live in—to see death as a natural part of living, and still, life must go on. I was relieved to return to work and back to some sort of routine in the New Year following the chaos of December. My days consisted of trips between the office, Cottage Hospital, and home. In June, I was certain my mother was going to die. Now I knew enough to be certain of nothing. It was rituals that kept me sane. Each time I left my mother, I kissed my fingertips and touched them to her forehead three times ... once for each of her daughters.

On January fifth, my mother was transferred to the Valle Verde Health Center and placed in an isolation room with another patient. Contact with my mother was limited over the next few days. Entering her room involved donning a paper robe, gloves, and a facemask. This provided very little comfort to either of us.

It seemed that Mom was able to rise from the dead once again. Although technically still in isolation, by the second day, she was up to her old tricks of toddling up to the nurse's station when her call light went unanswered. Within a few days, she was out of isolation and able to eat in the dining room with others. I hoped this would buoy her spirits and support her recovery.

Tuesday, January 9, 2018. I got out of bed, not feeling well after aches and chills during the night. The flu had finally caught up with me. I did not yet know that around 3:30 that morning, residents in Montecito were awakened by what sounded like an explosion. It was raining, but flames rose up the hillside. A massive mudslide then sent boulders down the canyon, ripping out power lines and crashing through walls. Some homes were buried, and others were swept from their foundations by torrents of water and debris. Cars and trucks were swamped in a sea of mud on the freeway, cutting off easy access by first responders. Twenty-three people died that night. The bright blue sky and billowing clouds the next morning seemed out of sync with the devastation that lay only a few miles away.

I spent the next two days at home and reached out to clients. I watched very little on the news that week. It was all I could do to manage my own distress to be present with clients and cope with an ailing mom. I learned the human impact of the disaster directly from my clients. One was a single mother with two children who had to be carried through the mud from their home by rescuers. She would spend the next several weeks moving from one temporary placement to another and trying to access the resources that were available. Santa Barbara was a community in shock and mourning.

When I returned to Valle Verde on Friday, I stopped to speak with Arleta, the charge nurse for that day. Arleta seemed cheerful as she reported that Mom was eating better now that she was back in the dining room. "Your mother is up to ninety-two pounds."

The tension in my body began to relax but returned instantly with what Arleta told me next. Earlier in the day, Mom had been watching a nature show on television in which a man was bitten by a snake. Mom was convinced that it had happened to her. All morning she had demanded to be taken to the ER. Finally, all ninety-two pounds of her shrunken five-foot frame hauled off and punched Arleta in the jaw as she cried out, "No one listens!"

My mind bounced between the image of my mother belting someone and my concern for Arleta. Arleta's response? "We've seen worse."

When I went to my mother's room, she tried to tell me about all sorts of strange things. She spoke with urgency, but her words were unintelligible—something about dipping water and streets. With my mind still on the snakebite, it was not until later I realized that she might have seen the news.

Later that evening, Mom's words were clear when she told me, "I don't expect to live ..." I listened closely as she went on to describe what sounded like otherworldly visions—but her thoughts and words could not meet.

I asked simply, "Is it beautiful there?"

"Yes," she answered, "but when you pick up the magazine, it dissolves, and no one else can see it."

There was a surreal quality to life after the mudslides—like the Salvador Dali painting *Persistence of Memory*, where misplaced clocks melt on the shores of an infinite dreamscape—the flow of curves against hard edges. A news video captured a car gliding down the canyon, lights and windshield wipers on. The natural beauty of Santa Barbara coexisted with images of crushed cars, destroyed homes, and the suffering of the displaced and the lost.

"Never Again."

Sunday, January 14. So much had happened during the week that I spent the day at home trying to catch my breath. It wasn't until late afternoon I headed over to Valle Verde for my daily visit.

When I arrived, I found my mother sitting in a wheel-chair outside the doors to the dining room. This was surprising ... she was usually up walking on her own—even when she wasn't supposed to.

I bent towards her shoulder and asked, "How are you doing?"

If looks could kill, her eyes were spitting venom.

"How do I look?" The tinge of disgust and bitterness in her tone provided the answer.

"Not good ..." I said gently.

Her eyes pierced mine as she said, " ... Never again!"

As the doors opened and the rest of the patients filed in to dinner, I found a perch on the corner of the couch next to her. She could be so clear in one moment and unable to express herself in the next. I wanted to understand what was happening ... As hard as she tried, I could not make sense of the words that came ...

I stayed with her awhile before rolling her into the dining room. I left with a knot in my stomach. Though her words had become scrambled, her message seemed clear—She was done! She was distressed, and she was angry! She didn't want to be here anymore—Don't f#@& it up! Don't interfere.

I went home feeling unsettled and returned that evening to do the only thing that I could do. I brought music to soothe the savage soul.

The next morning, I met with the social worker to find out the process for moving my mother back to Alexander Gardens and into hospice care. Afterward, I went to my mother's room with my computer and classical playlist in hand. I don't remember anything my mother said that day except for two words. She repeated the message, "Never again"—this time without the rancor of the night before.

As the melody of Beethoven's "Piano Sonata Pathétique" came on, my mother's head began to sway. Her delicate fingers picked out the notes on an invisible piano. As a child, this was one of the first pieces she ever learned to play.

I continued my daily trips to Valle Verde, usually before and after work. Sometimes Mom appeared fully alert. She could hold a conversation, but I wasn't sure she knew which daughter she had in the room. She asked how long I would be in Santa Barbara, even though I lived less than 15 minutes away. The mother that had witnessed the development of my career asked if I had a job.

At other times she lay propped in her hospital bed with her eyes closed. A slight smile would cross her face as she reached out ... not towards me, but towards whatever she was seeing. One morning when she was alert, she said, "You don't have to stay; the others are here." By "the others," I wondered if she meant the staff or those of another realm she seemed to visit.

By Wednesday, I'd put everything in motion to move my mother back to Alexander Gardens—only to learn that Dr. B was unwilling to prescribe hospice. The social worker said, "He doesn't think she needs it." Dr. B had not seen my mother in ten days. I did not know whether he was under the illusion that she was recovering—or he believed that it was too late. Memories of rocky moments with Dr. B jumped to mind, and I did not take the time to find out. I knew the value of hospice and proceeded with plans to move my mother to familiar surroundings—and to get a new doctor once she was settled.

A meeting was set for Friday morning at Valle Verde. A person from Visiting Nurse and Hospice would attend.

Most Precious Moment

When I entered my mother's room, a full team of caregivers surrounded her bed. There was a feeling of reverence in the circle around her. The team may have been doing some sort of ritual they practice—to ease the passing of the dying and perhaps those who have come to know them. If so, I wish that they had drawn me in instead of parting like the Red Sea. As they flowed out of the room, I was standing at the end of the bed. My mother's face looked peaceful and radiant.

Earlier in the week, each time I visited my mother,

she seemed less present. Her eyes were less clear—at half-mast. I come from a family of sailors who would understand when I say, "Her eyes were at half-mast ... the next day, the sails were reefed ..." On a sailboat, reefing reduces the area of the sail to slow the vessel in stormy seas. I never knew what those clouded eyes might mean ... I asked, "Do you know who I am?"

In the softest of voice ... the sweet curve of a smile on her lips ... she whispered, "My daughter."

I sat down on the bed next to my mother and lightly touched her hands and stroked her forehead. Her skin looked almost translucent. Even her silver-gray hair seemed to emit light. I felt like I was sitting with the innocence of a newborn babe. Free of the weight of history—hers and ours together. Unencumbered.

It was as if we were inside a luminous bubble. I was with my mother—but something else ... Pure essence ... Mom as spirit ... Something larger—an energy that joined us and expanded beyond. In this place, a thought came to me, "I forgive everything ... It's all up to me now." I am purposeful when I say, "A thought came to me." It had energy and direction. It came from behind the left side of my body and was without specifics, "I forgive this or that ..." It came without judgment or obligation. Perfectly clear.

A less wise part of myself felt that I needed to do or say something as part of our shared crossing. Quietly, I said, "You've had a good life ... you've done a lot ... given so much to so many people in ways that I don't even know ..."

Words felt inadequate and rang hollow in this space—perhaps unnecessary in this shared state of being.

Thursday, January 18, 2018. When I arrived Thursday evening, my mother appeared to be asleep. I was taken aback by a ragged sound emanating from her throat—as if she was struggling to draw breath. The words that come to me now are "death rattle." I did not recognize it as such at the time. The only word that came to me then was— *suffering.* As I look back now, I don't know whether my mother was suffering—I surely was.

I left to find Arleta. She came and sat next to me on the now empty bed directly across from my mother as we awaited delivery of comfort meds. I suspected the woman who'd lain in that bed before we sat on it had died. The chemicals used by the mop-up crew were so powerful they had burned holes in the rubber soles of my mother's shoes.

After we learned the medication would not arrive until nearly midnight, Arleta left to handle other duties. I stood and placed my computer on the tray table next to my mother's bed. The now darkened room filled with music. Though the comfort meds had not yet arrived, by the time I left, my mother's breath was smooth and quiet.

Friday, January 19, 2018. I arrived early Friday morning for the planned meeting with Visiting Nurse and Hospice. Valle Verde and Alexander Gardens had spoken and decided that my mother was too fragile to be moved. I trusted their decision, but did not fully understand what it meant. As naïve as it may seem, I did not know that my mother was dying or how quickly it would come. It's not that I was in denial ... I had never looked death directly in the eye before—and I didn't know that I was then.

I did what I had been doing for a long time—I put one foot in front of the other. I went to my mother's room before leaving for a doctor's appointment and then on to work … As I stood next to her, I was relieved that she was not struggling, but there was also a sense of emptiness. In the past, it had felt like she might leave and return, as she had done so many times before. Now it felt as if she wasn't really there. I lightly touched her shoulder with one hand and reached towards the sky with the other—as if I could build a bridge between my mother and beyond.

At the end of the day, I sat in my office across from a client with a serious history of childhood trauma. The pain of abuse often manifested as an intense fear of abandonment and rage toward her husband. As I heard the familiar pattern, I asked, "What would happen if you shifted your attention away from the story and into your body?"

The mind often holds a repetitive narrative about ourselves and the world. Awareness of bodily experience can open an entirely new landscape—of thought, feeling, and memories … and for this client—imagery.

I said very little as a picture began to unfold … First, she described a snake coiled inside her belly … spiraling upwards … ready to strike with swiftness and force. As we stayed with her experience, her body began to soften. She described feeling enveloped in warmth … and a love that felt to her "like the presence of God." The god-like figure then picked up the snake. "He's holding it up as if it is precious."

I marveled as anger transformed into love. She described the figure bringing the serpent to his cheek … then holding it tenderly against hers. As I watched, her hands curved next to her face, as if holding the now gentle creature.

I was mesmerized and felt as if we were inside a shared experience with no separation between us. I thought, "This is what it felt like to be with my mother ... Maybe she's here."

My client said, "I've never experienced anything like this before."

I replied, "Neither have I."

I left the office and went directly to Valle Verde, arriving just after seven. I stopped for a few minutes to talk with Arleta as she was coming out of my mother's room. She said she'd just given my mother her evening medication.

The lights were low when I entered the room. My mother lay perfectly still, her mouth open and her neck cocked back at a strange angle. I knew instantly—she was gone!

I called out to Arleta, who looked as surprised as I was. She had been with my mother only minutes before. Arleta checked for a pulse and a heartbeat—then confirmed what I already knew.

When Arleta went off to make the necessary arrangements, I was left standing next to my mother's body. Years before, I had been with a friend shortly after her father died. It had felt like he was still in the room, with light and energy surrounding him. This felt different. I touched my mother's hand. I tried to close her mouth, which opened again on its own. Her body was still warm, but there was nothing of my mother still there. It felt strange to leave, but almost macabre to stay. I gathered a few things, including her Memory Book, and left.

As I drove away, a dip in the road formed a womb-like hollow, with trees clustered on either side. The night sky and stars above created an empty stillness. There I remembered my mother telling me that when her mother died—she'd felt "more free."

It would take a while for me to find my wings.

REFLECTIONS

"Be patient toward all that is unsolved in your heart and try to love the questions themselves, like locked rooms and like books that are now written in a very foreign tongue. Do not now seek the answers, which cannot be given you because you would not be able to live them. And the point is, to live everything. Live the questions now. Perhaps you will then gradually, without noticing it, live along some distant day into the answer."

— *Rainer Maria Rilke*

Nothing Was as I Expected ...

There was no bedside vigil or weeping at the end. Our journey felt somehow complete.

There was still much to be done. When Ruth and Carolyn arrived from New York, we returned to the task of clearing. Objects that felt meaningful would become treasures in our own homes or find new purpose with others. There was no angst or conflict between us. All we had weathered together had drawn us closer. I had come to appreciate the unique role each of us played during the last years of our mother's life. Carolyn was the nurturer. Ruth was my problem solver, action taker, and sometimes mediator. As the "boots on the ground," I was the commander-in-chief, warrior, and water carrier all rolled into one. By the second day, Carolyn was felled by the flu and confined to a hotel room. Ruth and I finished the job.

It felt good to give. I gave David the patterned woven belt he coveted and first pick of everything we were leaving behind for the staff. He had earned it. I chose several necklaces for Bea—Mom's closest friend and mutual protector during her final months. Her friend Jean died during the flu epidemic, along with three other residents. Roderick, the Native American man Mom played flute with at Valle Verde, was performing oldies on his keyboard at Alexander Gardens that week. Ruth was able to gift Roderick with Mom's entire flute collection, to keep or to share with his students. The rocking chair that had been in our family since before I was born would remain in the respite room.

Mom would make her final trip East with Ruth—her ashes to be released into the Allegheny River, bordering Mom's hometown in Pennsylvania.

The Relationship Continues ...

After my sisters returned home to New York, I rummaged through boxes to find pictures Carolyn might include in the memorial announcement. As I sifted through the photographs, pieces of a life began to take shape—a whole person—a whole life. When I received calls from Mom's friends or encountered a neighbor in the grocery store, they shared what she'd meant to them. I began to see my mother through others' eyes, not only through those of a daughter. To this day, my understanding of my mother and our relationship continues to unfold.

My experiences with my mother have transformed my relationship with death—and my father. After my mother died, I had many questions I wished I could ask—and then it would hit me—she is no longer here. I knew that "life reviews" are common during the dying process, and I wondered, "Why wait?" Though living on opposite shores, I began asking my father questions about his childhood and experiences as a young man. My mother loved telling stories about her life when given half a chance and even wrote down a few. Much to my surprise, my father, too, enjoys sharing memories from his past—though he rarely does so unprompted.

With the arrival of Covid, most work and human contact went online. Our annual gathering at a beach in South Carolina was canceled, and our family began a new tradition. We now meet weekly for a family Zoom to share the happenings of our daily lives. Realizing I had an untapped resource, I began recording some of my private conversations with my father. People are always telling us what is most important in their lives, if we listen closely enough.

I now have the pleasure of getting to know my father in ways that I never have before. Because of my journey with my mother, my experience with my father will be very different when his time comes to pass.

"The Good Death ..."

During the weeks and months that followed my mother's death, whenever I thought of her, the words that came were, "Thank you." I returned to what I've called our "most precious moment" and the message that reached far beyond our bond: "I forgive everything ... It's all up to me now." Those became words I hoped to live by.

The "good death," the death I hoped for my mother, happened in June with her daughters at her side. Death had other plans, and its path was unknown—though clues were offered along the way. "I think I'll be around a bit longer ... I don't expect to live ..." Then, Mom's resolute instruction, "Never again."

Death became my teacher. At times I felt like I was fighting a battle that was not meant to be won. The specter of death confronts us with unsettling questions. When are we prolonging life—and when are we prolonging suffering? There are no easy answers.

There is no perfect death, only the best choices we can make in the moment.

We are constantly creating our lives through the choices we make. As difficult as it was, I am grateful to have shared this journey with my mother. Bearing witness to her aging, decline, and eventual death has prepared me for my own. Our shared crossing deepened our connection and strengthened family ties. The regret that remains is for the times I became so caught up in what needed to be done that I failed to see what she truly longed for. Me to be with her—simply present.

In life, as in death, pain and beauty are intermingled. When we accept death as a natural part of life, we can turn toward our loved ones and receive their offerings. In the words of my mother, "It's very special to be able to share what I'm seeing with you ..."

Opening to the experience of the dying is a gift to both. In death, we find the preciousness of life.

COMING FULL CIRCLE

"In the universe, there are things that are known, and things that are unknown, and in between, there are doors."

—William Blake

"Shared crossing" is a term that has come to describe extraordinary experiences that can be shared between the living and the dying towards the end of life. In this world, there is the slenderest of threads that separates life from death. A breath.

Life itself is extraordinary, and shared crossings, no matter how we define them, illuminate this truth.

Perhaps my most remarkable experience did not start with my mother, but began with my grandparents ...

Homer Riddle Jacobs, 1892 – 1975

Marjory Girard Jacobs, 1891 – 1993

January 1961 ...

Our family was visiting my mother's parents, Homer and Marjory, at their modest winter home in Florida. I was young then—young enough to believe that if I saved the fifty-cent piece my grandmother had given me, if it happened on a regular basis, I could buy a pony!

I was on the back-screened porch, trying to master the workings of a yoyo, when the phone rang. Even from there, I could feel the energy shift in the house as my father received news that his grandmother, Gertrude Galbraith Mildren, had passed. She died in her home in Weirton, West Virginia. A house my father knew well from his childhood. Like many couples with close lifelong bonds, my great-grandmother died only weeks after her husband.

Dad packed the family into our classic green Chevy for the drive from Florida to West Virginia. It was dark by the time we arrived at the funeral home. A soft glow of lamplight marked the path to the front door. I bounced up and down in the back seat, excited for the end of a long trip. Dad was going inside, and I wanted to go too. "I like her ... I want to see her!" At age six, I knew nothing about death, but quickly understood that I did not carry the right seriousness and solemnity for such occasions. I stayed in the car, still and quiet.

I find it both beautiful and strange what children remember. I'd met my great-grandparents only once, but it was a memorable occasion. My great-grandmother Mildren had a kind face—AND—a velvet-covered Queen Anne's chair! The intricately carved chair, in all its purple glory, sat on a landing on the staircase that led to the second floor. The noble face at its apex provided plenty of fodder for fantasy for a young girl while the adults talked below.

The next morning, I caught only a glimpse of my great-grandmother as she lay in an open casket. My sisters and I were neatly dressed for the funeral but kept outside in the hallway. During the service, we sat on a hard, wooden church pew. There would be no Queen Anne's chair with its soft plush seat that day ... Many years later, that mahogany and velvet-covered chair would become a treasured heirloom in my father's home.

1969 ...

I was a teen when my mother's father, Homer, had a debilitating stroke and never returned home from the hospital. As a child, I'd sat at Granddad's knee as he pulled the plastic wrapper from his cigar and handed the ornate paper ring to me. I hated the smell of cigar smoke but loved the ritual and small token of affection that came with it. In 1975, my grandfather died in a nursing home six years after his stroke. If there was a funeral, I did not attend. The man I remembered had been gone for many years. I was in college when my mother called to say he had passed. It was as if a wind swept through me—leaving an empty space. I knew some part of my life was gone.

1994 ...

Grandmother Marjory died in 1993 at the age of one hundred and one. A year after her death, I boarded a plane in

Los Angeles for a gathering of family and friends in the small town of Emlenton, Pennsylvania. A service and burial of my grandmother's ashes would be held on Memorial Day. The cemetery lies directly across the street from the white clapboard house my grandmother grew up in. The red-brick house next door was built by my grandparents and is the home in which my mother and her sister were raised.

During the flight, I studied the landscape below as the starkness of the desert turned lush green as we made our way east. I wondered what the next few days would bring. My family is a product of modern times—flung far across the country and sometimes the world. I was coming from Los Angeles, Carolyn from San Francisco, Ruth from New York, and my mother from Texas.

My sisters and I did not grow up close to our extended family, and events shared with aunts, uncles, and cousins were rare. That weekend, I would meet people who were important to me—though I had not seen them in many years. I had very little experience with death, and this was the first family funeral I would attend as an adult.

My mother, sisters, and I arrived in Emlenton a day or two before the memorial service. We stayed in a charming bed and breakfast that fit perfectly in a town that had changed little since our childhood visits. We decided to go on an adventure and drove out to the family farm that had belonged to my grandmother's brother, "Uncle Leon." I remembered visiting the farmhouse as a child. While my mother chatted with Great-Aunt Ida, I sifted through a box of buttons that looked like precious jewels to me. I was small then, and Uncle Leon seemed tall as we ventured out to see the animals.

The old farmhouse and the barn still stood—now in ruins. There was the occasional dish or old piece of clothing strewn about as relics from another time. The steps to the front door were rotten and would not hold the weight of anyone who tried to enter now. Still, the setting was beautiful. The house was surrounded by a field with old trees. Daffodils and blue iris had naturalized into a thick carpet of wildness.

As I circled to the back of the house to explore, I made a most curious discovery. Balanced on a single board that made up the back porch railing, I found an old leather-bound book open to a page near its center. This seemed strange—a single gust of wind could easily topple the book from its precarious perch. I studied the weatherworn pages that were open to a poem. As I came to the end, the final phrase read, "A little trust that by and by, we'll reap our sowing—And so, Good-bye!"

For a moment, I thought perhaps this was meant only for me—a clue to the meaning I was seeking that weekend. My mother picked up the book and began to close it. "No, wait!" I said, "I have to show you something." My mother, sisters, and I gathered to read the poem together. It felt important. It touched us all. This place and this experience meant—*family*. We ripped the single page from the book, leaving the rest.

That afternoon we returned to the farm and dug iris

and daffodil bulbs to take home to our own gardens. That evening we poured the earthly remains of my grandmother into a beautiful urn handmade by my sister Carolyn. We folded the poem and sealed it inside with my grandmother's ashes.

A few months after the memorial, my mother called to say she'd learned that the poem found at the farmhouse was part of my grandfather's high school graduation speech. I was dumbstruck by the news—and didn't know quite what to make of it. Some written parts of the service had been sent out to participants and those unable to attend. It was possible that someone had made the connection between my grandfather and the poem ... It was a great story—but more than 80 years had intervened—and I was not sure that it was true.

May the Circle Be Unbroken ...

2018 ...

After my mother's death, I was at the bank clearing possessions from her safety deposit box. I found her birth certificate, our family genealogy, and a page from the Emlenton newspaper dated June 16, 1910. There it was—the full commencement addresses of both my grandparents. The valedictorian speech was by an articulate young man—my grandfather. His address ended with the poem found so many years before on that porch railing:

A little work, a little play
To keep us going—And so,
Good-day!
A little warmth, a little light
Of love's bestowing—And so,
Good-Night!
A little fun to match the sorrow
Of each day's growing—And so,
Good-morrow!
A little trust that by and by
We'll reap our sowing—And so,
Good-bye!

What happens when we die? I have no answer to this most human of questions. I have only my experience from which others will create their own meanings.

In the end, I have no answers. I am left with only the mystery and wonder.

Classmates: We now bid farewell to our school, to our school mates, and to one another. Some of us perhaps will go on with our school work in other places, while for others this probably marks the close of school life. We doubtless will never again be united as a class, but memory will often recall the days of our struggles and triumphs together. May each of us so live that at life's close we may feel that indeed, "Labor conquers all things."

"A little work, a little play
    To keep us going—And so,
        Good-day!

A little warmth, a little light
    Of love's bestowing—And so,
        Good-night!

A little fun to match the sorrow
    Of each day's growing—And so,
        Good-morrow!

A little trust that by and by
    We'll reap our sowing—And so,
        Good-bye!"
                —HOMER JACOBS.

—It's your fault your corn hurts. Rexall Corn Solvent will relieve it at once. Gilmore's Drug Store.   adv

—When you want all the news subscribe for The News.

—Corn cure—Rexall Corn Solvent. Try it. Gilmore's Drug Store.   ad

DETECTIVE AGENCY

Bonded and licensed

This service is prepared to transact any legitimate business entrusted to it. It does not operate for rewards. Open day and night. Both Phones.

Emlenton News, June 10, 1910

APPENDIX:
END-OF-LIFE STUDIES

We, as humans, are meaning-makers. We have pondered death and imagined worlds that lie beyond since the beginning of history.

Swiss-American psychiatrist Elisabeth Kubler-Ross is the best-known pioneer of modern end-of-life studies. In 1969, her ground-breaking book, *On Death and Dying*, included the stages of grief and opened the discussion around death to a larger audience that has expanded into an ever-growing field.

Doctor Raymond Moody is known as the "father" of the near-death studies movement. The term "near-death experience" first became known to the general public in Moody's best-selling book *Life After Life*, published in 1975. Now a classic, *Life After Life* sparked more conversations, not only about death but also about the afterlife. Other authors include Peter and Elizabeth Fenwick, David Kessler, and Michael Newton, just to name a few. Moody's life-long exploration of what happens when we die continues in his 2010 book *Glimpses of Eternity* (with Paul Perry). *Glimpses of Eternity* focuses on what Moody called "shared death experiences." William Peters expands upon Moody's research on shared death experiences in his 2022 book, *At Heaven's Door*, which illuminates those experiences.

Near-Death Experiences (NDEs)

Near-death experiences provide a foundation for understanding unusual phenomena that may arise during a shared death experience.

Near-death experiences are stories told by people who have come close to death and then returned to life. The most common depictions of NDEs are of the dying person moving through a tunnel and towards a sublime light. In truth, accounts of actual NDEs are more varied. For example, the tunnel may be recalled as a portal or passageway—or described as moving through darkness—upwards towards or dissolving into light.

The "life review" is a common feature in near-death experiences. Scenes from the person's life are seen and felt, along with all their emotions—including awareness of the impact of their actions on others. Dimensions of time and space seem to bend. Memories may be experienced in rapid succession and/or simultaneously—all at once.

The senses are heightened during near-death experiences—colors seem more vibrant, and sounds may have unfamiliar qualities. Emotions are intensified. Many survivors say their near-death experience feels more real than everyday life—words cannot express what they have come to know.

NDEs often include sensations of lightness—including levitation and separation of consciousness from the body. Some survivors report "out-of-body experiences" during a medical procedure in which they were able to observe, see and hear everything that was going on in the room. Although they were unconscious or clinically dead at the time, some of the details may later be confirmed.

Some who have survived a near-death experience describe being joined by figures that seem to serve as guides—what some might call messengers, spirits, or angels. Many tell of being met by a single loved one or a greeting party—deceased relatives, friends, or others they have known during life.

Most survivors describe their experience as without fear or pain. Some tell of entering an indescribably beautiful realm—where they find a deep sense of peace, joy, and harmony. Others speak of encounters and conversations with religious figures or spiritual beings. The communication may be telepathic—without words.

Near-death experiences reach a turning point beyond which the person cannot go. Some describe making a choice to return to life. Others say they were turned back, told that it was not their time. Most express reluctance to leave the warm, expansive embrace of complete love and acceptance that they feel.

Survivors then find themselves back in the body once again.

People who "live to tell the tale" often express a deepened sense of compassion for others and an acute awareness of what is most important in their lives. Through their experience, they have gained a clearer sense of self, meaning, and purpose.

Not all aspects of NDEs are experienced as positive and may contain feelings of fear, grief, anguish, or shame. After their return to the world, individuals may struggle to make sense of an experience that is not easily expressed or understood by others. As a result, they often remain hidden—as stories left untold. Whether the near-death experience is blissful or challenging, the lives of survivors are forever changed.

Individuals' personal accounts of near-death experiences are accessible in books such as neurosurgeon Eben Alexander's *Proof of Heaven*, Anita Moorjani's *Dying to Be Me*, and surgeon Mary C. Neal's *To Heaven and Back*. Stories told by survivors can also be seen in Episode One of the Netflix series *Surviving Death*. This episode includes research by the Division of Perceptual Studies at the University of Virginia (founded in 1967), as well as some of the work of IANDS, the International Association of Near-Death Studies. A wealth of information on near-death experiences is available through other organizations, books, articles, and websites.

Example of a Shared Death Experience

With a bemused smile, a friend recently told me, "I had a strange experience with my husband as he died of heart disease. I didn't know there was a name for it." Anet and I hadn't seen each other for many years, but she began to tell me more:

> "The medical practitioners gathered up their things and left the curtained area. I was a bit stunned. While his death had been expected and talked about, it was still a jolt when it actually happened ... As I stood there looking at his body, my attention was drawn upwards to the far corner of the room where there were large utility pipes. And there he was, looking rather like the images of Casper the Ghost. He was laughing. As if to grab my attention, he started flitting about from place to place. He was a trickster. As an actor and theater director, this was so true to who he was. I started laughing too. For a brief moment, I wondered what people outside might be thinking, hearing the new widow laughing after the death of her husband. But that passed quickly, and I turned all my attention towards what was happening between Scott and I."

Experiences like Anet's are out-of-the-ordinary, but they are not uncommon. She went on to say:

> "Then, as if a veil was being lifted and a curtain drawn aside ... in the distance, I saw the backs of

two figures walking away from me and holding hands. They were walking in a very dry landscape, of sand and pebbles, with no vegetation. Large, rectangular chiseled rocks—like tombstones—were strewn all across the landscape. I realized that the two figures were Scott and I—and that we weren't husband and wife, or lovers, or father and daughter, but we were the best of friends. As the two figures continued to walk away, the scene faded, and the veil came back; the curtain closed. I was back in the ER with the body of my husband, and I began to cry."

A Card from My Father,
the Sailor ...

The obituary column of the *Sail and Power Squadron Magazine* is called "Crossing the Bar." It does not say whether the metaphor is about a boat returning to safe harbor after a life on the sea—or leaving the safe harbor and crossing the bar, going out to the unknown of the vast ocean. Many harbors have a bar at the entrance, which sometimes creates rough sailing as you cross. The metaphor works either way ...

ACKNOWLEDGMENTS

My deepest gratitude to William Peters, Michael Kinsella, and the Shared Crossing Project. Without participation in William's workshops, involvement in the research, and frank conversations with Michael, my experience around my mother's death would have been very different.

Many thanks to the people who inspired me without knowing it—Dr. Monica Williams-Murphy, author of *It's Okay to Die*, for her kindness when we met at the Family Therapy Institute and the very personal story she shared about her own experience with her father at his end of life. Thanks also to palliative care doctor Sunita Puri, author of *That Good Night: Life and Medicine in the Eleventh Hour.* I had the opportunity to meet Dr. Puri at a book signing. Her inscription, "Please write your story. It will help the world," kept me going when I wanted to quit. Thanks also to Dawn Montefusco, whose "One Short Book" course taught me that "short books are a thing."

Special thanks to Connie Josefs, an old friend rediscovered—and, as it turned out, an amazing writing coach and editor. Her memoir workshops helped free my ideas about what a memoir can be—several sections written in her class became part of this book.

Thanks also to Diane Adair, a good friend, wonderful actress, writer, and my first reader outside of my immediate family. Her brilliant suggestions furthered my editing process.

Deep appreciation goes out to Lisa Smartt and Paul

Perry of LifeafterLife.com, the website they share with Dr. Raymond Moody. Thank you for your interest and encouragement to become part of expanded conversations about the end of life. Thanks also to Lisa, author of *Words at the Threshold*, for her personal introduction to best-selling author Paul Perry. Deep gratitude goes out to Paul for his wise and generous mentorship and whose notes helped take my story to the next level.

My appreciation also goes out to friends, colleagues, and clients. The struggles they shared confirmed the importance of ongoing conversations about death and dying. Special thanks to my friend and colleague, Thery Jenkins, whose journey into end-of-life caregiving preceded my own. Our talks helped me to navigate rough waters when they arrived. Special thanks to my best friend from high school, writer and performer extraordinaire, Anet Ris-Kelman, who generously gave permission to share her shared crossing experience that appears in the Appendix.

My thanks to the team at Atmosphere Press: Kyle McCord in acquisitions; Alex Kale, Managing Editor; Tammy Letherer, Developmental Editor; Ronaldo Alves, Cover Designer; and Erin Larson-Burnett, Production Manager, for their support and guidance through the steps toward publication. Thanks also to BE Allatt and Chris Beale for their contributions.

Thanks first, last, and always to my family—my sisters Ruth and Carolyn—along for the ride in the fullness of this journey. My father for showing me what's possible during the latter chapter(s) of our lives. Special thanks to Carolyn as my first reader and IT helper, and of course, the rest of my family for their ongoing love and support, Judy, Howard, and Paul.

RESOURCES

Books:

Alexander, Eben, M.D. (2012). *Proof of Heaven: A Neurosurgeon's Journey into the Afterlife*. Simon & Schuster.

Chast, Roz. (2016). *Can't We Talk About Something More Pleasant?: A Memoir*. Bloomsbury Publishing.

Fenwick, Peter, Fenwick, Elizabeth. (2008). *The Art of Dying*. Continuum.

Gawande, Atul. (2014). *Being Mortal: Medicine and What Matters in the End*. Metropolitan Books.

Kessler, David. (2010). *Visions, Trips, and Crowded Rooms*. Hay House, Inc.

Kubler-Ross, Elisabeth, M.D. (2015). *On Death and Dying: What the Dying Have to Teach Doctors, Nurses, Clergy and Their Own Families*. 50th Anniversary Edition. Scribner.

Moody, Raymond Jr., M.D. (with Paul Perry). (2013). *Glimpses of Eternity: Sharing a Loved One's Passage from This Life to the Next*. Guideposts.

Moody, Raymond Jr., M.D. (2015). *Life After Life*. Harper One.

Moorjani, Anita. (2012). *Dying to Be Me: My Journey from Cancer, to Near Death, to True Healing*. Hay House, Inc.

Newton, Michael. (2010). *Journey of Souls: Case Studies of Life Between Lives*. Llewellyn Publications.

Peters, William. (2022). *At Heaven's Door: What Shared Journeys to the Afterlife Teach About Dying Well and Living Better*. Simon & Schuster.

Puri, Sunita, M.D. (2019). *That Good Night: Life and Medicine in the Eleventh Hour*. Viking.

Smartt, Lisa. (2017) *Words at the Threshold: What We Say as We're Nearing Death*. New World Library.

Williams-Murphy, Monica, M.D., Murphy, Kristian. (2011). *It's OK to Die*.

Documentaries:

End Game. Netflix Original Documentary. A Telling Pictures Production. In Association with Peer Review Films and Sidewinder Films. A Rob Epstein and Jeffrey Friedman Film.

Living with Ghosts: Science Tests After-Death Communication. Jenny Pictures. (Under option by PBS.)

Surviving Death. A Netflix Documentary Series. A Break Thru Films Production. Based on the book by Leslie Kean.

Films:

Away From Her. (2006). Directed by Sarah Polley. Starring Julie Christie, Gordon Pinsent, Olympia Dukakis, et al.

Still Alice. (2015). Directed by Richard Glatzer. Starring Julianne Moore, Kristen Stewart, Alec Baldwin, et al.

Still Mine. (2013). Directed by Michael McGowan. Starring James Cromwell, Genevieve Bujold, et al.

The Father. (2021). Directed by Florian Zeller. Starring Anthony Hopkins, Olivia Colman, et al.

Websites:

Shared Crossing Project
https://www.sharedcrossing.com

Life After Life
https://www.lifeafterlife.com/

University of Virginia Division of Perceptual Studies
https://med.virginia.edu/perceptual-studies

International Association of Near-Death Studies (IANDS)
https://iands.org/

B.J. Miller – Ted Talk – "What Really Matters at the End of Life"
https://www.ted.com/talks/bj_miller_what_really_matters_at_the_end_of_life?language=en

Metro, Rosalie. "When My Father Died, I Discovered the Unmentionable Stage of Mourning: Relief." Washington Post. https://www.washingtonpost.com/magazine/2022/12/05/when-my-father-died-i-discovered-unmentionable-stage-mourning-relief/

ABOUT ATMOSPHERE PRESS

Founded in 2015, Atmosphere Press was built on the principles of Honesty, Transparency, Professionalism, Kindness, and Making Your Book Awesome. As an ethical and author-friendly hybrid press, we stay true to that founding mission today.

If you're a reader, enter our giveaway for a free book here:

SCAN TO ENTER
BOOK GIVEAWAY

If you're a writer, submit your manuscript for consideration here:

SCAN TO SUBMIT
MANUSCRIPT

And always feel free to visit Atmosphere Press and our authors online at atmospherepress.com. See you there soon!

ABOUT THE AUTHOR

DEBORAH HARKIN holds a Ph.D. in Clinical Psychology with a specialty in Somatic Psychology and serves as a Marriage and Family Therapist at the Family Therapy Institute in Santa Barbara. Deborah brings a rich professional background encompassing social services, business, arts, and education. She has contributed to the academic community by publishing scholarly articles in the *USA Body Psychotherapy Journal*, based on her doctoral research on the adolescent brain. Deborah's passion for cultural diversity is evident through her extensive travels across Europe, India, and Southeast Asia. In her free time, she enjoys the study of history, the beauty of nature, and expressing her creativity through dance and photography.